Wo' Ton of the Blue Vision

Further Zen Ramblings from the Internet

Scott Shaw

Buddha Rose Publications

Wo' Ton of the Blue Vision
Further Zen Ramblings from the Internet
Copyright © 2018 by Scott Shaw
www.scottshaw.com
All Rights Reserved

No Part of this book may be reproduced in any manner without the expressed written permission of the author or the publishing company.

Cover photographs by Scott Shaw
Copyright © 2018 All Rights Reserved

Rear cover photograph of Scott Shaw
by Hae Won Shin
Copyright © 2018 All Rights Reserved

First Edition 2018

ISBN 10: 1-877792-16-0
ISBN 13: 978-1-877792-16-8

Library of Congress: 2018936304

Printed in the United States of America

10 9 8 7 6 5 4 3 2 1

Fade in:

Introduction

Here it is, *The Scott Shaw Zen Blog 10.0*, originally presented on the World Wide Web. All of the writings presented in this book were written between October 2017 and February 2018.

As was the case with the previously published volumes based upon *The Scott Shaw Zen Blog;* entitled: *Scribbles on the Restroom Wall, The Chronicles: Zen Ramblings from the Internet, Words in the Wind, Zen Mind Life Thoughts, The Zen of Life, Lies, and Aberrant Reality, Apostrophe Zen, The Abstract Arsenal of Zen, Zen and Again: The Metaphysical Philosophy of Psychology, Tempest in a Teapot and the Den of Zen,* and *Buddha in the Looking Glass* this volume is presented exactly as it was viewed on scottshaw.com with no rewriting, punctuation, or typo corrections. From this, we hope you will receive the original reading experience.

This volume of internet ramblings is presented with the date and time listed as to when each blog was originally posted. Also, the blogs in this volume are presented from last to first. With this, we hope to present a transcendence back through time as opposed to an evolving evolution. In addition, we left out the traditional *Table of Contents* in an attempt to leave this volume with a much more free-flowing reading experience.

Okay, there's the information and the definitions. Read on... We hope you enjoy it. And, be sure to stayed tuned for the ongoing *Scott Shaw Zen Blog @* scottshaw.com.

Wo' Ton of the Blue Vision

* * *
26/Feb/2018 03:14 PM

Have you ever noticed that whenever you confront a lair about lying they deny that they told a lie?

* * *
26/Feb/2018 03:14 PM

Jesus didn't write the Bible. The Buddha didn't write the Dhammpada. How do you know what they really thought?

What Gives You the Right To Be Angry?
26/Feb/2018 06:39 AM

Every now and then I encounter someone who bases their life upon anger. I have discussed some of these encounters in this blog over the past several years. But, whenever you meet someone who operates from that level, doesn't it make everything in life worse? Do you operate from a space of anger?

If you live in a big city, this style of behavior is more readily witnessed. I have discussed how I have watched people completely freaking out and yelling at me or other people in other cars just because they were in a traffic jam. What does that style of release truly provide? And, that is just one example.

Now, I'm not oblivious to driving anger. In the neighbor where I live, in the past few years, there has been a large influx of very wealthy people relocation from the Chinese mainland. Due to the fact that they, more than likely, never drove a car in the native country and then came to L.A., where everybody drives, they can really be a menace on the road. Combine this with the large elderly population that has lived in this neighborhood for decades and the roads, though they should be carefree, sometime are not. And, they are not for the most ridiculous reasons based upon poor driving skills.

But, as in all cases in life, it is how you deal with what you are given in life that not only defines you as a person but also creates the wake that you will leave throughout life.

As an example, yesterday my lady and I were taking an afternoon walk. We were crossing the street and this guy sees us but, none-the-less, turns the corner in his new Mercedes and just totally cuts us off. I put my arms like, *"What?"* I mean, in California, it's the law; pedestrians have the right of way. He sees me, puts on his breaks to intimidate me. This, of course, makes me smile. Like I always suggest, if you are going to break hard and pump up your chest with somebody you better first know who you are dealing with.

But, here lies the point... This guy was angry with me for him doing something wrong. From his anger, the situation could have escalated vastly and in a very negative direction. And, that's what anger does; it escalates.

A lot of people speak about the fact that they believe anger in our society is rising. Maybe? I don't know? I have witnessed it my whole life. But, the thing is, anger is noticeable. Anger creates situation that would not have been created if someone was not angry. Thus, as it does create situations, it becomes perceptible.

For example, if they guy had just driven courteously, like most people do, I would have nothing to write about. Or, if he would have waved a *"Sorry,"* I get it... We all make mistakes. But instead, he wanted to dig in his heals, become angry at a situation he created, and, thus, lead it towards possible escalation.

When you are angry—when you feel the emotion of anger, you really need to ask yourself why you are angry. Many times, in fact, most of the time, people become angry because they are not getting what they want. Life or people are not behaving in the way they want it or them to behave.

Now, I am not talking about the fact if some hurts you, steals from you, damages your stuff, or your life; then, there is a reason to be angry. But, undefined anger, helps no one or no thing.

So, I suggest, when you feel anger, get to its source. Figure out why you are angry. Take a look at the big picture of your anger; what feed into it and why. Next, look at the Life Positions of those you are angry at—try to see it from their point of view. And mostly, analyze how did you create the situation in your life where you decided it was time to be angry?

Anger is not a good thing. It leads to bad things. Know you anger.

Pot Shot People
25/Feb/2018 08:05 AM

For those of you reading this who may not be from the U.S., taking a Pot Shot at someone refers to shooting at someone from a hidden position where they can't defend themselves. This is a term coined by earlier generations that is not used too much anymore in modern colloquial English but it ideally depicts the way some people behave in life. They attack people from afar in a manner that leaves the attacked with little possibility of self-defense. You could also call this style of behavior a Cheap Shot, a Back Stab, or a Sucker Punch.

Recently, in this blog, I've been speaking a lot about human interpersonal interactions. Currently, for those of us who keep up with the news, at every turn, we are hearing about human re-empowerment via movements such as, #metoo, #timesup, #blacklivesmatter, and numerous other efforts that are designed to remove the power from those who have abused it. To a certain degree, I believe these movements have made a difference; at least on the surface. But, underlying the surface is always the layers of sediment that have originally given birth to a mindset of negative action taken towards other people.

As I frequently say, (and I know from the communications I have with you readers out there), I believe that most of the people who read this blog truly try to live a good life, make the world a better place, and hurt no one. They never take a Pot Shot. If they do hurt someone; like we all accidentally do, they apologize and try to fix the damage they created. They do not find their empowerment by taking pride in the taking control over and/or the hurting of others. They do not base their existence: financial, emotional, or otherwise, upon making money or gaining prominence off of the vision, the labor, or the artistic creations of others. They do not find joy in attacking or hurting other people. But, look around you; most people in the world are not like that. There is a horrible world out there where certain people choose to attack others—others who have no way to defend themselves.

Having been involved in the film industry for a lot of years, I have watched as the underlying conduits for getting a creative person's product out there grow rich while the true creators do not. This is especially the case in the independent realms of the industry. Why do these people do this and why can they do this? Because they the hold the keys to the kingdom—because they hold the money. Money made off of the creative vision of someone else. And, from that money they have the ability to buy attacks. Now, I have never been in that position of power but I have been on the receiving end of this style of attack. My defense; instead of fighting, deflect the negativity of the attack as best as possible. But, that doesn't mean it does not hurt. And, as I have long discussed in my martial art articles, deflection is virtually never the end-all to the confrontation as, if not fully disabled, the attacker may come back at you once again. Thus, a whole world of never-ending repercussions are set into motion.

This brings us to what this blog is all about. It is about you, the individual; what you do, how you do it, and what impact it has on other people. Do you take Pot Shots at people, from afar, based upon personal judgment, misaligned information, and/or the desire to control or hurt someone? Do you make money from this practice? Do you gain prominence from this practice? If any of these things are true, you are one of the culprits in the world. You are one of the people causing the damage. And, if you make money from this practice, what karma comes to you for every cent you take in?

Currently, in today's world, a lot of the BIG purveyors of bad-ness are being called to task for their actions. There are also a lot of unproven accusations flying around, spoken by people who are trying to find a way to the spotlight. But, in all of these cases, these people are in the upper echelon of society. But, what about us; down here?

The thing is, whether the people who are attacked or are attacking are right or wrong, few ever say, *"I did it; sorry..."* Instead, they find lies and excuses justifying their actions. They circle the wagons with those who support them. But, they never just acknowledge the truth of their action. They hurt somebody by what they did. Instead of trying to defend what they instigation, instead of trying to find away around the truth of what they did, instead of trying to find a justification for what they did, instead of trying to turn the blame on the other person, why can't they just say, *"Sorry,"* and set about fixing what they have broken?

Think how much better this world would be if people did not take Pot Shots. Think how much better this world would be if people did not try to justify their bad actions that hurt other people. Think how much better this world would be if people cared more about the other person than simply getting their hurtful actions and misaligned judgments unleashed. Think how much better the world would be if people cared enough about the other person to stop hurting people.

*   *   *
25/Feb/2018 08:05 AM

Everybody has an excuse.

* * *
24/Feb/2018 07:22 PM

You may want it for free but nothing is ever for free.

* * *
24/Feb/2018 05:06 PM

If you steal something from somebody you owe that somebody something forever.

Zen Filmmaking: The Final Definition
24/Feb/2018 11:04 AM

In the first exploration of Zen Filmmaking: 1992 until approximately 2005, the Zen Films were based upon character-driven dramas. Though always visually illuminating, by the mid-2000s, Scott Shaw began to redefine this Cinematic Art. Born, was the Non-Narrative Zen Film. These films initially held descriptions such as *A Zen Film Mind Ride, A Zen Film Meditation, A Zen Film Acid Flick,* and *A Zen Film Movie in the Moment.* In 2009, Scott Shaw created the last character-driven Zen Film. Thus, evolved was the final stage of Zen Filmmaking with all works being free of dialogue and focusing solely upon moving visual images and holding the titled, *"A Zen Film."*

Freedom of mind is the ultimate definition of Zen Filmmaking.

Why Waste Your Time?
24/Feb/2018 07:18 AM

Every now and then I will be strolling around the internet, looking for information about some subject or something like that and I will notice that there is some person trolling a person, place, subject, or thing. I mean, Wikipedia is ramped with that style of behavior. Some of these trolling sessions will be straight out lying libelous attacks. Others, will be complete nonsense for no apparent reason. And, in fact, some times, some body will be placing all kinds of praise on a person. But, whatever the theme, it always sends me to wondering, *"Why waste your time?"*

Back in the days of message boards on the internet, all kinds of nonsense was written. I mean, they are still out there, but not as prominent as they once were. There also were, and still are, to a lesser degree, sites where you can state your opinion, based upon nothing more than what you think or feel about some person or some thing. Facts be damned. But, it is put out there and presented as if it is a sociological piece of research. Now, some people believe all that they read. Thus, from this behavior lives are altered based on lies.

Sometimes, when I'm reading these troll attacks, I am actually impressed by how well they are written. In some, but not all cases, the person is truly a talented writer. And, this brings me back to the question of why? Why waste your time? It leads to nothing!

Now, I get it, we all sometimes just screw around on the internet. WWW: the world wide waste of time. It is like channel surfing—sometimes we just need to gel.

But, to go to these sites, with a purposeful message, based upon nothing more than internally developed boredom, angsts, anger, or love; I mean... Isn't there something more creative you could do with your time?

I understand the internet serves the purpose of giving those who wish to rise to the level of pundit the ability to publish their thoughts rather easily. I mean, it isn't that way in the actual factually based world of journalism. There, you gotta have qualifications! You gotta have substantiated sources! But, most of the people who are actually attempting to rise to a new level of knower are pursuing this dream in a more formalized manner for they know that what they say today may come back to haunt them tomorrow—especially if it is factually inaccurate.

...On a side note, at the university where I teach, I've known a couple of wild and rebellious university professors who lost their positions via posting biased and/or factually inaccurate information on the internet and I've also known of more than a couple of people who were never hired to academic positions due to their internet presence. Employers check that stuff now. So, what you put out there has gotta be right!

But, more than all this... I mean some people go nuts. They obsess over pages on sites like Wikipedia; claiming them as their own. Or, they attack other contributors. Maybe they keep going back placing false information (negative, positive, or nonsensical) on various sites around the internet. You name it... But, why? WHY! What does that give their life?

You know, for the most part, I imagine that these trolls are imaginative, creative people who have simple become lost in a mindset of doing the nothing that the nothing equals. This is not bad or good. This is simply a personal life choice. But, just think what some of these people could accomplish if they just got off of the troll mobile, focused, and actually pursued doing something BIG with their life. I mean, think of the things they could accomplish...

And, for those of you who have fallen prey to this type of behavior; stop it! Stop focusing on what has already been done—on dead people or people who are old enough to be your parents or your grandparents, and/or on subjects you have no control over. Get out there and do something original. Why waste your time?

Sorry
23/Feb/2018 07:07 AM

Most people are not sorry about anything that they have done unless they are provided with a reason to be sorry.

As you have passed through your life, how many times has someone done something to you that hurt you, damaged your life, altered the next step in your existence, or taken something from you that was very important to you? When those occurrences have happened, how many times did the person care enough to realize what they have done, try to fix what they have damaged, replace what they have stolen, and say that they are sorry?

The concept of sorry does not naturally exist in the minds of most people. The reason for this is that people operate from a perspective of <u>me</u>. …All they think about is themselves: what they are feeling and what they desire. The concept of the greater whole is actually feed to a person when they are continually told that is how it should be. This is certainly the case of family. As a family unit, one is constantly reminded of their interconnectedness. Thus, it is much more commonly, within the bounds of a family, that when one does something that negatively affects another member of the family that they will apologize. Though this is not always the case. Many people have created great riffs in their family unit that once created are never repaired. Why? Because one person cares more about themselves than anyone else.

Within the realms of a family there is a certain need to repair damage that was inflicted upon a close relative. Due to the common proximity within a family, if a resolution is not achieved then constant conflict is given birth to. Here, we find the first example of the statement, *"Most people are not sorry about anything that they have done unless they are provided with a reason to be sorry."* As they are in a family, as other members of the family are urging them on, they must find a resolution.

In your life, how many times have you been hurt by a family member? How many times did the family member that hurt you apologize?

Once you step beyond the realms of a defined cohesive unit like the family, a reason to feel sorry becomes more distant, however. Certainly, the closer you are, on a personal level, to a person that has injured your life, the more common it is for them to care enough about you to apologize and attempt to fix what they have done that hurt your life. But, take just a few steps away and it is rare that any person has a consciousness refined to the level that they will actually care enough to even take notice of what they have done to the life of another person. That is, unless they are forced to.

Maybe this force comes in the form of being arrested for what they have done. Maybe they are sued in a court of law. Maybe they have the shit kicked out of them in a physical confrontation. But, without some intense motivating factor, it is rare that anyone cares enough about the person that they have hurt to apologize.

Have you been hurt? I have. I believe we all have. Hopefully there have not been too many of those instances in your life.

From a personal perspective, as I have been in the public eye for much of my adult life; due to the books I have written, the movies I have made, etc., (all be it in a very small way), I have watched as some people have damaged my life from afar. Did they care? Obviously not. In fact, it may have given them some sort of misplaced interpersonal joy and a sense of accomplishment.

People behave in this manner due to any number of reasons but one of the primary ones is that they do not care enough to understand that each person is a human being with the same feelings, concepts, and understanding of reality that they possess. As the person they go after is someone out there in the distance, they are not real. This is the same mindset that goes into someone who steals something from some person. The person who steals is not evolved enough to care about the fact of the emotional impact what they are doing will have on the person they are stealing from. For those who attack people, they seek to find personal empowerment and domination and they do not care about the results of their actions on that person unless they are caught and prosecuted. Then, the world, *"Sorry,"* is used in abundance.

As we pass through life, it is undoubted that we will be hurt by the actions of other people. It is also true, that more than likely, we will hurt someone else. Whether this action was an intentional act or not, the results are the same; we have hurt someone. Thus, as a person choosing to live consciously, a positive and compensative action must be taken.

As I always say, there is one person who is the initial instigator of any action that is set into motion. They choose to do something. If they choose to do something that hurts another person, no matter what their motivation; they are the culprits. Thus, it should be them who sets about to disengage their initial action, repair the breakage when possible, and say, *"Sorry."* Can you be that big and that whole of a person to do that? Can you care enough about another human being to do that?

Life comes at us from all angles. We all want the same thing: to be happy, to be loved, to live a fruitful, prosperous life, and, mostly; not to be hurt. With this as a basis, we must realize that all people are the same—they all want the same thing. From this, we must each strive to never hurt anyone, say, *"Sorry,"* if we do hurt someone, and fix what we have broken.

Think about it... Wouldn't this make everything just a little bit better?

* * *
22/Feb/2018 04:11 PM

If you could erase one thing that you did in the past what would it be?

What Do You Believe In?
22/Feb/2018 07:33 AM

What do you believe in? Everybody believes in something. Maybe it is God, Jesus, Allah, The Buddha, Nature, Dead Ancestors, or Spirits from the Great Beyond. Or, maybe you believe in nothing. But, believing in nothing is believing is something.

Here is the question, *"What does what you believe in cause you to do?"*

Take some time to think about the answer to that question.

Many people find a reason to do things that are not good for the greater whole of humanity and the world based upon what they believe.

Many people seek forgiveness for what they have done to others based upon what they believe.

If what you have done, based upon what you believe, has hurt even one person, what you believe in is not based in the betterment of all people. Thus, what you believe in is not a good belief.

Think about what you believe in before you do the things you do in life. Think about why you believe what you are doing is okay. Think about who and what your actions will affect, both positively and negatively, before you do what you do based upon your beliefs.

If you have hurt even one person, based upon what you believe, you have hurt one too many people.

Zen: Conscious Interaction or Interaction Consciousness
22/Feb/2018 06:53 AM

Here's the intro for a book I began writing a couple of years ago but got distracted and never finished.

Life is about consciousness. Life is about consciously living. The more consciously you live your life, the more refined understanding you develop about the inner working of yourself, human kind, the universe, and god.

Most people spend their entire lifetime driven by unchecked emotions and desires. They run from wanting to anger about not getting what they want. When they get, they are happy for a moment but then they want something more and from this they are no longer content. Thus, they are again driven to disharmony and rage about not having all that they desire. Though this is a common thread that runs through the life of many/most people, this is the ideal example of a life defined by lack of consciousness as there is nothing conscious about desire, wanting, and rage.

Everyone wants what they want. This is an element of the human condition. This being said, the consciousness individual, the person who walks the path of consciousness, does not let desire and/or emotions control their actions and reactions to the world around them. For if you do, that means you believe yourself to be the center of this universe; which you are not. If you do live your life by this code, however, by doing so, you do whatever you deem necessary to get what you want. But, by living your life in this manner, you injure the lives of all those around you. This is never the path of consciousness.

Many people are falsely feed the belief that if they ask for forgiveness, if they do something good, then their wrongs are righted. No, this is incorrect. Yes, at some point an individual who has wronged others, driven by the own emotions and desires, may experience remorse for their actions, but the only doing is the undoing of anything bad you have done but this is impossible in this Life Space. What you have done is what you have done and though you may seek forgiveness for your actions; your asking forgiveness from a religious elder or some divine entity never can change what you have done. Thus, the person, persons, or the Life Space you have damaged, remains damaged.

People wanting gives birth to lying. People wanting gives birth to damaging actions. People wanting gives birth to bad behavior. People wanting never gives birth to refined consciousness.

In this world people seek. They seek possessions, they seek position, they seek power, some even seek enlightenment. But, the common factor and the incorrect element to this equation is, *"The seeking."* For at the very root of seeking arises the desire for things to be different than they already are. At the very root of seeking is born the concept of unhappiness due to not having. From this, all the damage to others, all the damage to the earth, all the damage to the all and the everything is given birth to.

At the root of Life Betterment is consciousness—focused human consciousness. As humans, all we can be is humans. As humans, we are defined by being human. This being said, it is the person who chooses the path of refining their consciousness that <u>consciously</u> eliminated as many of the negative obstacles of human existence as possible; namely: uncontrolled desire equaling rage, equally lying, equally power-grabbing, and power-tripping. From this, the damage unleashed onto others is minimized and the world becomes just a slightly better place.

In this pages of this book life, life occurrences, and actions will be detailed and discussed. From this, each who read these words may be able to learn from experiences that they did not have to live through but were able to witness; lived by the life of others. From this, new understandings of better way to live life and react to life may be understood. From this, a more conscious world may be born where you, personally, may have the chance to become a more wholly fulfilled and conscious Live-er in this Life Space.

* * *

21/Feb/2018 12:32 PM

If you wipe your countertop with a dirty rag does your countertop become any cleaner?

* * *
21/Feb/2018 12:29 PM

Why do you want to make someone/anyone your enemy?

* * *

21/Feb/2018 12:28 PM

Are you whole enough to move yourself beyond your opinion?

Influencing the Masses
21/Feb/2018 09:23 AM

Recently, I think all of our attentions have been brought to the subject of Fake News. Certainly, the news media is riddle with this term; both discussing it and being accused of it. But, what does this Fake News actual do to society?

I remember when President Obama was elected and I would be in the presence of staunch Orange County Republications. Some of the false statements they were making about Obama were unbelievable. Yet, they heard them, they believed them, and they said them. Thus, the lies got bigger and bigger.

Certainly, if someone was aware enough to actually study the facts, they would not be swayed by what these people were speaking. But, the fact is, people seek out their own kind—they rise to their own level. Thus, if negativity is what a person embraces and that is what they are driven by; that is what they will find.

With our current president, Trump, this spreading of Fake News has not subsided. It has just flipped to the other side of the coin; from conservatives speaking their falsities in the Obama era to the liberals doing it in the Trump era. But, the essence of these false truths are just the same. They are not true.

There is an elemental problem when people spread their opinions as facts and speak of what they have not faculty authenticated. That problem is, the speaker messes with people's lives. They may be saying what they think, they may be saying what they feel, but if what they think and what they feel is not based upon fact, all they do is add to the mess of propaganda this world has become based upon.

Many people, as they pass through life, seek distractions. These distractions come in many different forms. Some, particularly the young, as they do not have to make a formalized living to keep food in their belly and a roof over their family's head, turn to the words of others to find direction. If the direction they have found is disreputable and factually inaccurate, then they have based their entire existence—what they will do next in their life, upon a lie. ...A lie spoken by someone else.

Everybody has their reasons for saying what they say. Everybody has their reasons for thinking what they think. But, what is the essence of those activities? If it is based in truth, then all is well with the world. But, if it is based upon provoked negative opinion—defined by someone who never substantiated their facts, then all of the world is set in a downward spiral.

Facts are facts. Opinions are opinions and are oftentimes false.

What do you think? What do you speak? Why do you speak what you think? And, what is the repercussion to the life of one person and/or the entire world who listens to what you say based upon what you think?

Get the facts first! Speak the facts only!

Helping Those You Can Help
When You Can Help
21/Feb/2018 07:42 AM

One of the key themes of my life has been always been helping people. No one told me I was supposed to do it. I just always wanted to help those people who needed help. But, some people who need help, you cannot help.

It is important to note that most people do not want to help others. They want to judge, criticize, and attack. They especially want to do this when they are at distance from those they are confronting. Some even feel that critiquing is helping in that they have affixed their negative appraisal to a person and/or their actions. This is not helping. As I say over and over, hurting is never helpful.

For those of us who actually do want to make a positive difference in the lives of those who do need help, there is the natural desire to run to the rescue of all those in need. The problem is, in certain cases, helping may actually cause more problems than it will help. So, we have to be conscious and careful.

Let me give you a few recent examples in my life where I choose not to step in, when I wanted to. And, it was probably for the best.

Recently, I was walking through the outdoor central area of this city center. There was a young man just going off; angrily screaming all kinds of stuff about nothing. This, when there was a lot of people around. Looking at him, I could see that he probably was not schizophrenic or psychotic. Instead, as he was very sweaty, he was probably tweaking. Seeing the ruckus this guy was causing, this guy on a bicycle stopped and said, *"Why don't you go and sit over there in the shade and calm down."* The screaming guy immediately angrily came back, *"Is that a suggestion or a commandment?"* Then, the back and forth began... I walked away. The guy was high, you were not going to help him with words. All words would do would be to escalate the situation and give him more fodder for his anger. Drugs are bad!

A few days ago, I was about to cross this street. I don't know what it was but everyone was driving very fast and very crazy on it. The light changed and I began to walk across it. This lady in her SUV, barring down the street, goes right through the red light. Though she was several feet from me, I yell, *"Hey!"* Just about at that moment, I hear breaks screeching. Another SUV almost hit this young woman. The young woman was with a guy who darted to the other side of the street. The girl stood there for one of those long seconds in front of the SUV staring at the driver. He did not nothing. Did not get out. Did not say, *"Sorry."* Nothing... She finally moved to the sidewalk and fell to her knees. I get it. That's traumatic! The driver dove off. The girl's friend gave her no sympathy. Inside of the store where we were all heading, I saw the girl walking around with tears in her eyes. I get it! I thought to go up to her but I did not want to be the creepy old guy coming up to and talking to a young woman that I did not know as that may have weirded her out more. But luckily, she had made it through the event; more or less safe and sound. I wanted to make her feel better. But, what could I do that would change the events that had just taken place?

Recently, I was in one of the stores I frequent. Walking around, I see this twenty-something girl sitting on a chair. She had a mirror in her hand and she was staring deeply into it. Immediately, I could see that she was tripping on Acid—seeing all those things in that mirror that could only be reveal to her altered mind. She smiled at me. I smiled at her. Actually, I always smile at everybody. One of the shop girls I know, who works there, came up to me and said that the girl had been there for a couple hours. The staff knew about her presence, realized she had taken, *"Something bad,"* as she described it. But, they were just going to let her sit there as she was harming no one. That was nice I thought. There was certainly a part of me, having experienced that mindset myself, that wanted to help the girl and maybe get her to a more positive place to hang out. But, where would that be? Where could I take a young woman that was tripping on Acid? So, I smiled at her again, just to check on the condition of her trip. She smiled at me and I walked on.

Here's the thing in life, most people only want to help the most obvious of candidates. That is, if they want to help anyone at all. Maybe you give the homeless guy, asking for some money, a dollar or two. Or, maybe you tell them to go get a job as I have witnessed many a time. But, people need help all around you. The old, the young, the weak, the strong, the poor, and the rich. And, you should help these people if you can. Be strong enough to step up to the plate, even if the greater crew in that arena are for the home team when you are not. And, that is perhaps the best definition of when to help. When all the voices are against the one; the one person or the one situation. For if the one is surround by support, they probably don't need help. It is the one on the outside of the conglomeration that needs your aid.

      Give help when you can help. Raise you voice for the person being attacked. Give help to those who need help. Be strong enough to turn against the crowd and reach into the life of the person who needs assistance. Do so, unless as described above, the person has survived and your helping them may only cause their current standing to worsen.

      Never hurt. Do good things. Say good things. Be strong enough to help.

* * *
20/Feb/2018 07:21 AM

What do you do with your thoughts when you wake up in the middle of the night?

Losing Your Destination
20/Feb/2018 07:17 AM

As we each pass through life, there will be location that we truly come to love—places we really like to go to. Some of these will be outdoor locations: maybe a beach we really love, a place in the desert, a park, or a specific area of the mountains. Though these locations may have lived uninterrupted for eons, once the hand of man (or woman) became involved, they are changed and perhaps even eradicated.

The physical places we like to go to are for less likely to live through the centuries, however. The shops, the restaurants, the bars, the galleries, the coffee houses, the pool halls, the gyms, the you name it… As they are dominated solely by the whims of society, their life span can be expected to be far shorter. And, this is sad! Don't you hate it when a place you really loved goes out of business? …The longer you live through life, the more common this occurrence is going to become.

I have lamented about the disintegrating world of bookshops more than a few times in this blog. As a lover of books, with the recent and rapid ever-changingness of how people receive their information, so many GREAT bookstores have fallen by the wayside. One of the most recent ones to bite the dust was Logos up in Santa Cruz, California. Man… I loved that place!

Logos opened in '69. I discovered it in about '73. Whereas, The Bodhi Tree, here in L.A., (also gone) really helped to walk my young mind through the spiritual path, Logos did that plus provided me with an endless supply literature, poetry, and cultural studies. I have read a lot of books. ☺

For those of you who may not know, Santa Cruz is about three-hundred and fifty miles North of L.A. and about eighty miles South of San Francisco. Way back, in the way back when, it was a hot bed for Eastern Spirituality. Whether I went up there every couple of weeks or every month or so, Logos was always there. Whenever I was in the city, I went there and always found something new and great to read revealing new understandings.

More than just a place to buy things, these locations we love are a place to interact. I certainly realize, that as cultural has become introverted; with its face lock into computer or phone screens, human interaction has greatly diminished. But, that is sad. Actual, face-to-face, human interaction is all we really have in life. It is the only true definition of life. It is the only way to come to know and understand life. …Though, I understand, many have lost sight of that fact. But, personal interaction is the only way to know people and understand humanity. And, bookshops were a great way (at least for me) to meet people of like mind.

For each of us it is different. Where we go is based upon what we have learned about life and what we want from of life. And, when we lose our destination a little part of our self is taken away. Sad, but his is life… See you in my memories Logos…

Stop Doing Bad Things
16/Feb/2018 02:21 PM

With the most recent school shooting that took place this week, it is once again bought to our attention how what one person does can destroy the lives of so many people. The news is saying that this is the deadliest school shooting in U.S. history. And, that is just sad!

Many people speak about the escalating culture of violence in our country and in the world, but I don't know if that is true. Throughout my lifetime, I have watched as violence has been unleashed throughout all cultures of the world. Whether it was the Vietnam War, the Killing Field of Pol Pot, the discriminatory actions of groups like the KKK in the South, the assignations of people like JFK, Bobby, MLK, or John Lennon, or the jihad that is currently in-action in the Middle East; mass-scale murderous violence has gone on throughout my lifetime and if we look back through history, it has gone on forever. Growing up on the wrong side of the tracks, I witnessed it daily in my schools and in my neighborhood. Though gun possession was not so prevalent among the teenage set when I was young, there were other methods and other weapons that people used to inflict pain and/or death.

The thing is… And, though people want to talk-and-talk about what should be done to stop all this violence, very few people look to the way they, personally, are behaving and how what they do affects the greater whole of the world causing violence to be unleashed.

Violence is usually spurred on by one person. The fact is, some people take pride in their ability to instigate anger in others and then have that anger directed towards one person or a group. But, should that person be allowed to feel joy in the hurting of someone or something else? I believe the answer to that question is, *"No."*

Moreover, some people once they have hurt someone, choose to deny the damage they have caused with every breath. Or, they attempt to justify their actions. But, hurting anyone or anything for any reason is wrong. And, that is what has set this culture of violence into motion.

I think back to a person who lived across the street from one of my friends many years ago. He was Scottish, so he and I had a certain connection. I remember one Saturday my friend and I were hanging out and he came over. We asked what he was up too. *"Just beating the wife,"* was his answer. And, he was serious. Now, instead of feeling guilt or remorse for those actions and/or maybe trying to seek out therapy or anger management treatment he, instead, was looking for people to cheer him on—to tell him that what he did was okay. Of course, we did not. But, what he did illustrate is how violence can begin on the personal level and then spread outwards either being accepted by or being disseminating to the masses.

What do you do in your life? Do you judge people, do you say things that make people angry about other people and other groups than the one you belong to? Do you actually say or do things that causes people to become agitated or angered at one person or one thing? If you do, that means that you are an instigator. As an instigator, you are responsible for any negative action to other people or places that your words set in motion. As you were the provocateur, it is your karma.

Now, the fact is, everybody wants to deny their personal responsibly in anything negative that happens to someone or something that originated from them. ...Though, as detailed, there is a small group of people who actually take pride in their negative instigations. But, the truth be told, if you said something that caused someone else to do something that hurt the life of anyone for any reason, you are one-hundred percent responsible for that instigation.

Are you HUMAN and ACTUALIZED enough to accept that fact and either undo what you have done or repair the damage that you have inspired? Most people are not. But, that does not make what they have done justified. And, whether the words equaling those actions were large or small, this is what initiates and reaffirms the culture of negativity and violence that is going on in our world. You are responsible for that. Own it!

As we saw in the recent school shooting, though there may have been a million-contributing factors, one person did one thing that hurt a lot of people. Though you may not possess a gun and go out and shoot people, what you say and what you do has just as much potential to hurt, maim, kill, and destroy the lives of other people. Choose to be more. Choose to stop the violence that your words and your actions have the potential to unleash. If you have hurt someone be strong and whole enough to fix it. And, hurt no-one any-more.

Max Hell Frog Warrior: Where's the Nudity?
16/Feb/2018 09:30 AM

I received this question the other day and I thought it might be something that some of you out there may like to know the answer to, as it is not the first time it was asked.

"Hi Scott. I found this old magazine and it showed pictures of you with a couple of seminude girls talking about shooting your movie Toad Warrior. I've seen Toad Warrior and Max Hell Frog Warrior but there are no nude or seminude girls in it. What happened? I always like the nude girls you and Donald Jackson put in your films for no good reason."

To answer… Don and I were torn between having nudity in Toad Warrior AKA Max Hell Frog Warrior or not. There was one side of us that wanted to use nude females. As Roger Corman so aptly said, *"Nudity is the cheapest special effect."* And, it's fun. The other side of the issue was, we were debating whether or not we should make Toad Warrior a more family friendly film. Me, I was good either way…

We did do a few publicity photo sessions with nude and seminude actresses during the filming of Toad Warrior. We also shot a few scenes having seminude actresses participating. In the end, however, we decided to go the other direction and keep the film PG. Whether or not that was ultimately a good or a bad decision, I can't really say. Nudity turns some viewers off. But, as the questioning party just stated, he, among a lot of other people, like it. Though, I get it… Gratuitous female nudity is totally politically incorrect in this day and age. Anyway, it was the choice we made,

and we had to live with it. Hope that answers the question.
 FYI

Honoring What is Honorable
15/Feb/2018 09:20 AM

Everybody knows what is good. Everybody knows what is bad. Everybody knows what is right and everybody knows what is wrong. The problem is, many/most people do not look to this innate knowledge that exists within themselves and allow it to guide them through their life. Instead, they find sustenance, motivation, egotism, and power by doing what they internally understand is not right. From this is born a personal mindset, expanding to a culture, where doing the wrong thing becomes acceptable.

Hurting is wrong. Have you ever been hurt? If you have, then you know it is wrong.

Stealing is wrong. Have you ever had anything stolen from you? If you have, then you know it wrong.

Saying bad things about people is wrong. Have you ever had someone say bad things about you? If you have, then you know it is wrong.

Lying is wrong. Have you ever been lied to? If you have, then you know it wrong.

These are just four of the very basic things that people commonly do. There are obviously many more. Though people know, at their inner core, that doing these things is wrong, they do them anyway. They find a reason to do them, which equals a motivation for others to do them. Thus, BAD is given birth to. Thus, people's lives are damaged and the entire world is engulfed with negativity that leads to ongoing bad action(s).

What are you going to do about it? Are you going to personally stop yourself from doing bad things—things that you know are wrong? Are you going to stop supporting and cheering on people who do bad things that you know are wrong?

The world begins with you. Your life begins with you. What you do and what you encounter begins with you. And, all things good are given birth when you honor only that which is honorable. Stop the bad. Stop doing bad things.

*   *   *
15/Feb/2018 09:16 AM

Are you viewing your life only from the spectrum of today? Or, are you viewing if from the spectrum of tomorrow?

Do you look to your past to see what brought you to today? Or, do you forget all those who added to your discovery?

* * *
15/Feb/2018 09:16 AM

How many people do you associate with that you don't really like?

On the Inside Looking Out
14/Feb/2018 07:45 AM

Here's a flashback essay for you. I originally composed this piece maybe twenty years ago for a magazine and I just came upon the original text. It can also be found in my book, *Zen: Tales from the Journey.* Enjoy!

When one thinks about those who walk upon the spiritual path, the idealized image of an individual wearing long robes with a shaved head or a sadhu with long dreadlocked hair and an unshaven face is commonly the first thought which comes to mind. These external images of apparent holiness sets those who live in the modern world to somehow believe that an individual is not truly holy if they wear normal clothing, shave each morning, and get their hair trimmed one a month.

When I was an adolescence, forging my way on the spiritual path, I sent a letter to the modern American guru, Ram Dass. I posed him a few questions, which my adolescence mind believed to be very important at the time. Though I was not sure that someone so seemingly holy as Ram Dass would have the time to send me an answer, a month or so later, a reply did, in fact, come in the mail. Yes, a letter from the man himself. As I read his handwritten words, I found that it was not just a reply but I also received a personal invitation to meet with him at a gathering he had scheduled in the Los Angeles area the following month. My youthful mind was awh struck.

The day of the gathering arrived and I made my way to the location. I walked into the room and there he was, Baba Ram Dass, the man who the media had made mythical. I was somewhat set back, however, as he came up to happily greet me. I realized that he wore common slacks and a pull over sweater. Somehow, I had expected him to be wearing the traditional clothing of a Yogi: a dhoti and a kurta. Or, at least, the cotton drawstring pants which were common place for the era. I mean, all of my friend on the spiritual path wore pseudo Yogi clothing. Why didn't he?

This erroneous mindset is the perfect example of that possessed by many of this modern era. Holiness is gaged by external appearance. By how a person looks, not by how they live. It is for this reason that so many people play, *"Dress up."* They somehow believe that if they wear the robes of a monk, have the dreadlocks of a sadhu; that if they appear holy, they must be holy. But, this is all folly.

There is an amusing story which details the other side of this issue and describes how a person who is not walking the spiritual path perceives one who is.

When I was in my third semester of college, I had already long been living the spiritual lifestyle. As such, I had been initiated into the order of sannyas and was wearing the orange clothing which delineate my standing. (Not orange robes, just orange clothing).

My collegian friends would just call me, *"Swami,"* as most of them couldn't get their tongues around the longer version of the spiritual name I had been given. They were all supportive of my path, however, commonly asking questions; as strange as I may have appeared.

I was taking a class on philosophy, which at that time was my major. The instructor was an aging professor, who was one of those people who projected the mindset that they knew everything and the students knew nothing. He was obviously much different from my previous college instructor on the subject of philosophy who was a Vietnamese Buddhist monk.

We took our midterms. Though academic Philosophy is about as far from the root source of the word as one can get, I, none-the-less, believed I had done okay on the exam. When the tests were returned the following class meeting, I was presented with the grade of *"F."* Down the side of my paper was a paragraph long discourse on why I had received the grade. *"You cannot be a Swami, you are too young. You do not know enough. You will never know enough. You are Caucasian, not East India, etc., etc., etc..."* There was, however, no comment on my actual essay answers.

At the time, this attitude shook me. Having surrounded myself, from a young age, with those walking the spiritual path or those who were my close friends and were very accepting of my chosen vocation, I had never encountered this style of prejudice.

The grade I received made my classmates quite angry, however. Much more angry than me, as I was locked into the pseudo spiritual space of, *"It all is as it is. It is all perfection..."*

When I left the class that day, I wondered how I was even going to pass the course if I was to be judge by how I looked, not by how I performed. This brought to mind the questioned which had been posed to me many times, *"If I was walking the spiritual path, why even bother attending a university?"*

For me, education was about learning for the sake of learning. Though being spiritually innocent is a benefit, being uninformed seems to serve little purpose. Though the established educational institution are certainly not the only pathway to schooling, for me it seemed the appropriate road.

As I walked across campus mentally debating the occurrences of the day, I thought back to a time a year or two the previous—I was going to the store to buy some supplies for a spiritual community I was involved with, the Integral Yoga Institute. I was standing, waiting for the light to change on Sunset Boulevard in West Hollywood, when these two girls from the Midwest drove up. Seeing my long hair, long beard, prayer beads, and funny clothing, they asked, *"Are you a Hippy?"* I laughing answered, *"No, I'm a Yogi."*

When I returned to the center, I told my story to one of the sisters of the order She said, *"See Shiva Dass, God was testing you."*

On the spiritual path you make a choice everyday. You can choose to follow the ways of the world. Or, you can choose to follow the divine order of the universe and be spiritual.

This understanding certainly has nothing to do with how you are dressed, however. But, how dress will delineate how you are perceived.

The Sikh wears a turban. This tells the world of their religious conviction. The Priest wears a collar. This lets everyone know of their profession. But, does what a person wears truly depict spirituality? No, it does not.

External is always external. External can never be internal.

What you wear for clothing can tell the world something about the life you choose. It can even influence how you behave—if you are seen as holy, you may behave in a more spiritual fashion. Though all of this may be seen as an aid to spiritual progress, in actuality, it truly is not.

External image also leads to ego. The monk who wears robes is immediately assumed to be and treaded as a holy crusader, just as the military officer who wears a uniform is immediately seen to be a trained combatant and is treaded accordingly. To truly embrace spirituality, you must transcend the need to be defined by your external image.

The modern teacher, Bhagavan Shree Rajneesh, though he became seemingly lost in the power of his position as his years as a teacher progresses, his original teaching, none-the-less, possessed a very pure understanding of universal suchness. He believed that if a person wished to renounce the world, even for a moment, he would provide them with the method to do so. This was the basis for what he called, *"Neo-Sannyas."* And, explains why he had so many followers who wore orange clothing and possessed the title of Swami.

This ideology is very true. If you can simply renounce the world for a moment, the rest of your life will be altered for the positive. If you can let go of your desires: let go of caring who you are, what you are, what you are to become, and how the world perceives you, even for a second, then in that moment of freedom, you can touch Satori.

It is essential to remember that spirituality is not defined by what you wear or who you are on the outside. Spirituality is about who you are on the inside.

It took me awhile, but I left behind my orange clothing. It took me a little while longer and I left behind the Sanskrit names and the yogi clothing—though this was not before I received a *"D"* in the class from my all-knowing philosophy professor, who was the perfect example of the fact, perception are the basis for Maya. And, Maya is the pathway away from Satori. As long as you care about how you are perceived, you cannot perceive your true Buddha Nature.

Let go of perceptions and the world will be a much better place. Let go of excuses, forget about how a person, situation, event, or even yourself appears. Move past the external, embrace the essence of nothingness. This is Zen.

* * *
13/Feb/2018 10:44 AM

If you are doing something that hurts somebody you are doing something that hurts somebody.

Where does that place you in the spectrum of life?

∗ ∗ ∗
13/Feb/2018 06:52 AM

How do you know that I exist?

* * *
13/Feb/2018 06:49 AM

It is not how fast you read what you read, reading is about how well you comprehend the words on the page.

* * *
13/Feb/2018 06:49 AM

If someone doesn't care, there is nothing that you can do to make them care.

What Is The Definition Of Your Life?
12/Feb/2018 07:13 AM

What is the definition of your life? Who are you? What are you? Take a few moments and consciously calculate how you would define yourself.

For each person this definition is different. A person may define their life by so many factors… It may be their family, their children, their job, their age, where they went to school, or what they do in their spare time. For others this definition may be based upon a more egotistical standard: their looks, where they live, the car they drive, or the rank or position that they hold. Some people define themselves by what they do; either by positive or negative means; *"I help others,"* or *"I am a killer or a thief."* What about your personality? Are you vain, judgmental, caring, or forgiving? And, are you honest with yourself? The main constant in all of these definitions is that most people never take the time to ever think about who they are and to actually formally define what they have done and what they are doing with their life.

It is essential to note that the definition of Self by Self is a definition based upon the ego. It is how you see yourself and how you hope to be viewed by the world. But, how do other people view you? Take a moment, turn off your Self-Definition, and a think about how other people characterize you. Think about how your family views you, how your friends see you, how the person you do not know that you pass on the street would define you. Be honest with yourself. How do the people you have helped view the help you gave them? How do the people you have hurt view what you did to them and how do they see you as a person?

Most people are very proud of the positive aspects of their life: the things they own, the things they have achieved, and the positive contributions that have drawn them accolades. Most people try to hide the negative aspects of their life; if they have stolen, lied, killed, cheated, were an addict, chosen to receive an abortion, given up a child for adoption, or were a bad person, doing bad things, in all of those ways that is defined by society. Though many hide from these factors by lying or denying, many of these negative factors are what actually define who that person is—though what they have done is not known by the greater whole of the world because they hide it.

Who you are, defined by yourself, is how you move through your life. The things that you are proud of and broadcast to the world and the factors that you hide from the world all add to the definition of you. How consciously conscious you are is what allows you to take control over yourself and your life and guide it in a positive direction that not only makes you a better person but keeps you from damaging yourself, your evolution, and/or the life of other people.

Take this time, right now, and define who you are, what you are, and why you are. Learn from it so you can alter and possibly change the negative aspects of you and what you have done and, thereby, embrace the positive aspects of you, so you can rise into the best example of you that you can be. Remember, your definition of you is only half the equation. How other people view you also adds to your ultimate life description.

In unbiased honesty there is truth and all truth begins with you being truthful with yourself.

* * *
09/Feb/2018 01:10 PM

What you do, you choose to do.

What you do becomes a habit.

What do you choose to make your habit?

Your habits define your life.

Beefin' in the Streets
09/Feb/2018 12:35 PM

So… I was having breakfast at this outdoor café this morning and about five or six men were having a heated discussion. Don't you hate it when you are just trying to chill and people drag you into their melodrama? I mean, I just wanted to enjoy my coffee and breakfast and look at cat photos on Instagram.

It kept going on and on with one of the guys noticeably getting very agitated. *"I'm not going to get involved in that! No way! It's your own fault! That's just wrong!"* Etc., etc., etc…

Now, I guess I should describe these people as that will add to the overall story. They were of Middle-Eastern heritage. Most had the long bead with no mustache. One wore traditional garb. From their dialect, I could tell they were from the Sindh region of Pakistan. They veered between their native language and English. The agitated guy was the only one of the crew who stood out due to the fact that he was very tall, heavyset, and intimidating looking.

Apparently, what was going on was one of the men, the clean-shaven guy in the well-pressed button-down shirt, (there's always one of those in these deals), was having business problems and was trying to bring together these other people, who had obviously invested money with him in the past, to give him more money to instigate a new hustle to keep him afloat.

I cannot tell you how many of these kind of deals I have witnessed and have heard of. In the film industry, it is all over the place. I mean the hustlers, hustle. They live their life based on hustling money from other people. They do that, until they can do it no more. The stories I could tell you... I've even watched as one person hustled their own mother out of her house so they could sell it just to keep themselves afloat for a little while longer. Their mother ended up homeless and destitute. That's just bad... You may ask, *"Who could do that?"* But, people do... And, they always have a reason; they always have an excuse for doing what they do when they take what they take from someone else.

 I say this over and over and over again, but no one ever seems to listen to me until it's too late for them. If you are basing your life and your livelihood upon taking things from other people, (whatever that thing may be), sooner or later the well is going to run dry, people are going to get angry at you, and your world will come crashing down on you—crashing down on you hard. That is just the nature of the beast... When you take, you owe!

 It's kind of like this one song from the '70s comes to my mind whenever I hear about or witness this type of situation. It's by a band named, Uriah Heep, the song is called, *"Stealin',"* and the lyrics go, *"Stealin' when I should have been buying."*

 And, that's just the reality of life! So many people find so many ways to make their money—to make their living off of the labor, the creativity, and the resources of others. But, it's all just a hustle. They do it until they can do it no longer and then they grapple at straws trying to keep themselves afloat, promising anyone they can, that it will get better soon and to help them out—help them out while they continue to hustle other people and take from them no matter what the cost is to that person they are talking from.

Finally, the big guy started yelling, *"Fuck this,"* and stormed off. He was pissed. The hustler, in the button-down shirt, tried to chase after him but one of the other guys stopped him. Which was probably a good thing.

By this point, I had finished my breakfast. I got up to leave. As I walked by, a couple of them had remained with the main hustler talking the prospects of the hustle. Hustling someone else…

Now, this kind of mindset is all over the place. The film industry, the entertainment industry, the real estate market, the banking industry, the used car market, the stock market, you name it… There is one person (or more) trying to hustle money out of the pockets of another person. …Get it from them so they can do what they want with it. …So, they can live the kind of life and lifestyle that they desire all based on what someone else has actually generated. Get it, with no care what it costs that person who gives it. And, it's not just money; people steal all kinds of things so they can make their bank to live their life all based on what they took from someone else.

All I can say (again) is don't do it. It will come back to destroy you.

Me… Basically, those people totally ruined my breakfast. That's what they took from me. Thanks a lot…

Pierced Ears
09/Feb/2018 08:23 AM

I was watching this Hong Kong Action flick last night, from the grand era of Hong Kong Action—prior to the Chinese takeover. One of the scenes had a couple of the characters running through this one shopping mall. Having spent a lot of time in Hong Kong in the 1980s and into the 1990s, I knew that shopping center very well. In fact, I had a couple of the many holes in my ears pierced at that shopping center one upon a time. This made me smile with the memory.

Having always been closely aligned with counter-culture, I first got my ear pieced when I was thirteen. Back then, if you were straight, you pieced the right ear, if you were gay you got the left one pierced. Look to any performers of that era, like Prince, and you will see the one solitary earring in the right ear. But, also being deeply involved with Eastern Religion, and seeing how all of the male gods had both ears pierced, I was one of the first men, of this new era, to have both ears pierced. Men didn't do both ears back then. But that, one on each side, quickly became not enough for me. I popped a bunch of holes in both of my ears.

This brings us to Hong Kong 1980 something??? I was in Hong Kong waiting for my Chinese visa to be processed and I ended up walking through this aforementioned shopping center. There I saw this very pretty girl sitting behind a counter that offered ear piercing with the purchase of earrings. I don't know if it was the petty girl that drew me in or the thought of needing something different, but I walked up and asked her to do my ears. We did our business and I sat down to get my ears popped.

Now, this was the only time I had ever had my ears pierced with one of those ear-piercing guns. Prior to that, it was always done by my girlfriends. So, this was a new experience.

Anyway, I was being all-smooth, the way a single guy does when he likes a girl; hoping she liked what she saw and would notice I was wearing an Armani suit and a Rolex. …You know, how Hong Kong is all about the externals… Anyway, just as I was about to start up the conversation, she goes into this whole rant about how I had too many earring, why do I have so many earring, and how bad all of those earrings look on a man. Then, she goes off on my hair. *"Why is your hair so long. You look like a girl…"* Anyway… Obviously… The communication session did not go as I had hoped… ☺ But, I did get a new hole in each of my ears.

Thank you Hong Kong Ear Piercing Girl for the memories. I wonder where you are now?

What Happens When You Cause Somebody to Commit Suicide?
09/Feb/2018 08:17 AM

In life, there is the instigator and the receiver. There is the attacker and the defender. There is someone who decided to do something to someone for some reason and once it is done it is done. But, the attacker is left the attacker while the defender is left picking up the pieces of what the attacker has broken in their life.

Once something is broken it is near impossible to fix. Drop a cup on the ground, watch it break, and then try to glue it back together. It will never be the same. Life is very much like this; people say things and people do things that hurt other person and they do this with seeming impunity. In fact, many take pride in what they say or do that leaves a person's life broken and damaged forever.

How many people who say or do negative things actually care about what they did or the overall affect they had on another person's life? If they do care, they commonly only can about the pride they feel in hurting someone else.

It is not uncommon to hear about a young person who commits suicide due to the ongoing taunting from one person that may then spread out farther to the masses. One person said or did something that damaged their life but then that break in their life became the defining factor of their life and it hurts so bad they can take it no more.

When you look to this person's life, many will say, *"Why couldn't they be stronger,"* or *"Why couldn't they find help or support?"* But, in some cases, it is not that easy. Sometimes what one person negatively instigates causes a mountain to fall on that other person and they believe there is nowhere to turn, and it will never get any better. Thus, they take their own life.

Does the person who is at the source point of the instigation care or feel bad about the person or what they did to the life of that person? I suppose that is different in each case. But, whatever they feel, it does not remove what they instigated. They said or did something to some person which caused that person's life to be altered forever and caused their destiny to be tarnished. Thus, leaving that individual with the perceived understanding that there was no other alternative, no other salvation, but to take their own life.

Most people do not say or do things that causes another person to take their own life. In fact, some people are very good hearted and try to help humanity. But, others may focus on one person or do something negative to everyone they meet. They find their target, take their focus, and hit the person in a manner where they truly hurt their life and when that person can find no support or retribution, they are forced in the direction of ending their own existence. They do this instead of living a life defined by emotional misery. The karmic pointer is obvious, but the end result is that one person did something that hurt someone else; the person on the receiving end ended their own life, while the instigators lives on to possibly to do other things to other people. Is that right?

To the original question, *"What happens when you cause somebody to commit suicide?"*

You decided to say or do something, you took that person in your crosshairs, you did what you did, and you hurt their life so badly they died because of it. All fingers should be pointed at you but because of life placement they probably are not. Certainly, if what you did was a physically illegal act, you may end up in jail. But, many of the things that cause people to take their own life are much more subtle than that. It is the ongoing experienced pain they emotionally feel on the inside. And, if they are constantly reminded of this pain, by the various means that are out there in this day and age, and they can find no peace and no new life to live, then they fall into a space of desperation. When this desperation is amplified by solitude, anxiety, and ongoing despair, they do what they do to try to survive but they should have never been lead down this road in the first place as there still remains one instigator who is responsible for all of the emanations of the actions that came next.

All life is your responsibility. What you say and what you do in life is your responsibility. You can do good things. Or, you can do bad things that hurts other people.

Loving or hating someone else is never a reason to hurt them. For those emotions are simply based upon your perception of another person's reality. Meaning, they are not right or wrong; they are simply your perception. With this as a basis of understanding, you should never judge, attempt to define, or hurt anyone else based on what you think about them. Because you do not truly even know or understand who that person is or why they do what they do. At best, all you are doing is judging and from judgment lives are ruined. You could be next on the chopping block.

Be more than the person who instigates negativity in the life of anyone.

            *   *   *
            08/Feb/2018 01:59 PM

Somebody popped this up on twitter a couple of hours ago. Thanks for letting me know. From my book, *About Peace*.

Is peace something you get, or is peace something you are?

If you can get it, you can lose it.

If you are it, it is never gone.

* * *
08/Feb/2018 07:37 AM

Until you've lost someone or something that you truly love due to their death, you do not have a true perception of life.

*   *   *
08/Feb/2018 06:50 AM

Was the melodrama you created worth it?

The Way of the Word
08/Feb/2018 06:49 AM

I was doing a commercial yesterday. As it was a big union gig, when it hit the appropriate time, they called, *"Lunch,"* so the cast and the crew headed for the roach coach.

Personally, when I working on a film or any other cinematic project, I don't like to eat lunch. Small or large production; I feel like it slows me down and takes away my mental focus. And, I don't generally like the chitchat and the small talk that takes place on the sets during lunch. But, as mentioned, it was a union gig, so the rules must be followed...

While the people were eating, I looked at my Yelp app and found a nearby thrift store. I thought I would go and check it out, as you never know what you will find.

Anyway, I drive over and I'm in the store looking around when this woman walks up to me. Very presentable and very coherently she begins to speak with me. She references this one person, like I know him, and that she is going to meet them at this church that does a lot of charity work. She goes on to say that once there she will prey with the man. Then she exclaims, *"And oh, by the way, I'm Jewish..."* Okay...

Initially, I thought that she had me mixed up with someone else, as she was so rational. But then, I begin to realize that all may not be as it seems... I smiled and told her, *"I have no idea what you are talking about..."* But, she continues. She goes into this whole discourse and though the words were all very well chosen, they made absolutely no sense.

To conclude our conversation, I told her that she sounded great and that should really go and do a spoken word performance. With this, she referenced Bukowski and god. Me, I smiled and walked away.

You know, it is kind of interesting... Word are such an important defining factor of our existence. Most of the words that are spoken are expected. You know what will come next. But, there is another level to all this. Certainly, in the late fifties and into the sixties, there were some great wordsmiths who began to alter our understanding of how one word should precede another. From the Beat Generation, we got notable people like Burroughs and Ginsberg who really put a new spin on sentence construction. This trend, of course, continued, throughout all levels of poetry. And certainly, way back in the way back when, the Haiku started the rearrangement of word synthesis.

But, back to this moment—here was this person... If she was a poet, if she was at a spoken word event, like I suggested, she would be praised. But, in reality, she was just bat shit nuts.

It is an interesting point to think about when reading words; poetry or otherwise. Why do we say the things we say in the way that we say them? Why do we only understand things when they are placed in an expected syntactic pattern? Why can't things be new, different, revolutionary? And, do you have to be crazy to actually to be able to chart new realities with words?

Not a Victimless Crime
08/Feb/2018 06:48 AM

We are coming to the end of the 2018 Awards Season. As I am a voting member of the Academy and the Screen Actors Guild, SAG/Aftra, I have recently watched a lot of movies. Some have not even yet been released. These films were all provided to me by the studios and they were, *"Industry Only Screener Copies."* Before you can view them, you must click that you agree not to duplicate, share, copy, or sell these DVDs. Sure, that's all on the Honor System. But, honor is what life is all about.

Once you have agreed, you are then shown all of the FBI Copyright Warnings. One of them says, *"FBI Anti-Piracy Warning: The unauthorized reproduction or distribution of a copyrighted work is illegal. Criminal copyright infringement, including infringement without monetary gain, is investigated by the FBI and is punishable by up to five years in federal prison and a fine of $250,000."* Another says, *"Piracy is not a victimless crime."* Strong statements.

As a person out there in the real-world, (maybe you are a filmmaker or maybe you are not), but do you actually believe any of those words. Do you believe you will go to jail and get fined if you make a copy of a movie? Do you even think about whether or not, *"Piracy is not a victimless crime?"* Do you even care? Do you care about the filmmaker? Do you care about the filmmaker getting paid for his or her creation? Or, do you just care if like or don't like a movie and/or that you got it for free?

As a filmmaker, I personally have seen the downside of what can happen when somebody steals your film. I have talked about this a lot in this blog and in articles and books I have written about the subject. But, the fact is, you people out there probably do not care. You want it for free and once you have it, you want to do what you want to do with it. If you want to copy it, put it on the internet, or pull it apart and critique it; you want to do what you want to do. Some of you even claim Fair Use. But, Fair Use is a complicated, ever-evolving doctrine. And, as I have said before; the law is the law and the moment you make one cent off of someone else's creation, in a court of law, that is a Copyright Violation and Fair Use goes out the window. But again, do you care? Hey, you'll never get caught. Right?

There is also a whole other side to this issue. For example, a couple of people have brought to my attention that recently some people have been complaining about the audio quality of one of my early films, Roller Blade Seven. The fact is, the audio quality on that film is very good. Very good if you are watching an authorized release. The copies where the audio is bad are the unauthorized releases or the bootlegged copies. And, that's just one example of what you get from a pirated version. They are not the intended release version!

You know, making a film is not an easy task. Whether you are making it with a few hundred dollars or millions upon millions of dollars, at each level there is a lot of obstacles to overcome. Out of respect for the people who actually care enough to make a film—care enough about the cinematic art form to get out there and personally do it, you should respect them and their creative energy enough to not illegally download it and/or use their creation for your own end goal. Whether you love or hate a film is irrelevant. ...Believe me, there were a lot of films this season that I did not like—and that is the same every year. But, I respect the creator(s). I respect what it took to get that film made. I respect the process. And, I honor the system. I do not steal or make money off of someone else's hard earned artistic vision.

Think about what you do before you do it and the consequences it will evoke not just to you but to the actual filmmaker. Mostly, care enough to care about the people that care enough to create.

The Anger That Lingers Inside
07/Feb/2018 08:18 AM

Have you ever had a friend that you thought you could trust and then, out of the blue, all of sudden, they did something that completely messed up your life? Has there ever been someone out there in the far reaches of your existence, someone you didn't even really know, and they do something to you somehow/someway that truly messes up your existence? But, why does this happen? Why do they do it?

People do what they do for any number of reasons. It is impossible to climb into their mind and truly understand their motivation. In fact, most people are not in-tune with themselves to the degree that they could truthfully tell you why they do what they do when it comes to doing something negative to someone else's life. But, there is one generalized truth and that truth is, if a person was content with themselves, if they were satisfied with their own life, if they did not hold deep seeded resentment towards another person based in jealously or anger, if they did not seek adoration, they would not hurt a person. In fact, they would do all they can to not hurt that person.

In my life, I have watched as certain people have done things to me. These are people that I believed were my friends. Yet, motivated by that unsubstantiated whatever, they did something that damaged my evolution. In some cases, they denied what they did. In other cases, they lied about what they did. Some justified what they did. And, in still other cases, they ran and hid.

I have also watch people I know do negative things to other people. ...Do things that a true friend or even a person with any sort of actualized conscience would never think about doing to someone else. Yet, they did it and their action truly hurt that person's life.

In some cases, people take pride in hurting someone else. They take pride in the damage they have caused. They feel they possess the intrinsic right or the established knowledge to hurt that person. Then, they find all kinds of justifications for why they did what they did. Some may even gloat about what they have done with their friends. But, at the end of the day, hurting only hurts. It never produces anything positive.

So, here we are… We are left with living a life where we must embrace other people and, in some cases, believe them to be true friends. But, the fact is, some people are not a true friend at all. Something in them will click when they are given the opportunity to lash out and they will hurt you. It's not right but it is the way it is.

This is the same with the people out there on the extremities of our existence. As these people have no close, personal relationship with us, to hurt us holds no immediate repercussions. Thus, they do not even possess the ability to think about how their actions are going to negatively affect the life of the person that they are doing what they are doing towards. This is not a conscious way to live a life. But, think about how many people you have encountered who operate from that perspective.

As a person who has been involved in the fighting arts for most of my life, I long ago realized that the most dangerous person to fight is someone who does not care—a person who has nothing to lose. For a person like that fights just as the description implies; they have nothing to lose.

Many people operate their life based upon this precept. As they have nothing to lose, there is nothing you can do to hurt them if you counterattack. Thus, they will do what they do and no matter how angered you may become at what they have done, they will not care. So, seeking an apology or wanting them to undo what they have done or provide a fix will never happen. They will simply live within a space of either being proud about what they have done or a mindset of not caring about the damage that they have caused.

      A person, who will do things to hurt you, is not a true friend; no matter what motivation they may claim. A person who will do things that hurts someone they do not know is only motivated by a mindset of selfishness and not caring. For hurting anyone, for any reason, has no true justifiable logic. But, we are surround by people like this every day of our life. Hopefully you will be lucky and never encounter a person (friend or foe) who possesses the ability to damage your ongoing life-evolution. But, if you do, what can you do? I don't know… I guess it is different in each case. You can try to deflect and protect yourself. But, once the damage has been done, the damage has been done. And sure, karma will come to get them; someway/someday. Hopefully you will be around to see it. But, hurt, hurts. All you can try to do is find a better place with better people that will care enough about you to take your mind way from your pain. In the meantime, I guess the best thing that you can do is to go out and do something good for someone else. At least with this action it will make something in the greater everything just a little bit better.

* * *

07/Feb/2018 06:58 AM

Your life is defined by what you do with what you have.

* * *
07/Feb/2018 06:57 AM

If you want to keep secrets don't be in a relationship.

Isn't That What Art Is?
07/Feb/2018 06:52 AM

I always find it interesting when people dismiss another person's art. Maybe they say it's terrible. Maybe they say, I don't like it. Maybe they even say it isn't art and the artist is no true artist. Curious…

From time immemorial, there has been the first person to do the first thing. Almost universally, that first thing is not liked or appreciated. As we humans have climbed our way through the centuries, there are those who have fallen in line and become a part of the greater whole and there are those who have stepped outwards and explored new realms of understanding. In some cases, this has been within the realms of art—art by whatever form it may take. These people, these explorers, these artists have quite commonly been criticized.

Think about art a century or so ago. Based in realism, it had become very formalize, very defined, and very accepted. Then, there came to be a few people who pushed the boundaries of that accepted art forward. By the mid-twentieth century, abstract art had moved into the main stream of consciousness. Today, go to any expansive art show and it is filled with what may be defined as varying levels of modern or abstract art. Thus, what was once shunned has become mainstream. The generalized masses may not still particularly like that style of art or they may falsely claim that, *"Anyone can do that,"* but it is known. Thus, though it may be beautiful, the people who create it, break no new ground. They simply use that method as a means of personal artist expression.

At the heart of any true art is one person taking a concept that they envisioned in their mind and making it a reality. For some, yes, they expand upon what has come before them. For others, they simply take what it is their mind and truly push the boundaries of understanding forward. Are they loved for it? Is their work appreciated? Most commonly not. At least not during their lifetime. Mostly, it only provides the critics with something to dismiss and poke their judgments towards. But, none-the-less, what these people are instigating is a new level of understanding. They are creating art as they envision it. Thus, they are the true artists.

Two Sides of the Story
06/Feb/2018 08:56 AM

There is the old saying, *"There is always two sides of the story and the truth lies somewhere in the middle."* In some ways, this is true. Some people operate from a very self-centered perspective. They know themselves, they know how they feel, they know what they want, and they do what they do based upon what they think they know, what they feel, and what they want. Add to this a position of power or empowerment and if the individual is not, by-nature, a thinking and considerate person, selfish actions are given birth to. Thus, there is the person doing the doing and the other person who is on the receiving end.

We can say forever and ever that people should always be considerate of the other person. We can say forever and ever that people should think about the other person first. But, in the lives of most people, this is rarely the case. People get locked up in their own projection of reality and they rarely take anyone else in consideration when they set about doing what they do. Again, add to this the sense of empowerment or power that some people receive due to their position in life, and then, instead of simply not thinking about the other person, they demand things from that other person.

Certainly, in this era of #metoo and #timesup a lot of these situation have been brought to light. I too have discussed a couple (but not all) of the situations where I have been on the receiving end of power manipulation in my life and career in this blog. So, it can happen to anyone.

If you have been on the receiving end—if you have been forced to do something you don't really want to do; well, welcome to life. I do not believe that there is any person who has not had to do something they did not really want to do in life. They have had to do this to get their degree, get a job, keep their job, stay in a relationship, and the list goes on. But, it all comes down to the fact that what you have chosen to do to develop or maintain your relationships or your lifestyle, you later regret. Again, welcome to life. It happens to all of us.

Perhaps this is where the source of the problem begins—at least on the larger scale of reality. We all want our life to be the way we want our life to be. Some people are more understanding that it may not always be that way, however, while others refuse to have anything other than the way they want it to be. From this, is born a life where we are forced into doing things to guide us towards our end goal and, thus, a life where conflict is eminent. From conflict, there is always damage. From damage is born resentment, hatred, and the desire for retribution. Thus, there are two people, doing what they do; each basing what they do upon doing what they do for a prescribed set of reasons, thereby equally a life where there are two people telling two entirely different stories about the same subject based upon two completely different perspectives and motiving factors.

As I often discuss, in life there is always one person who sets a situation into motion. They are the one who has decided to do something and if that something involves another person then they are the one who is ultimately responsible for what comes next. Though they may deny this fact till the end, they had an idea which led to an action which led to affecting the life of someone else. Thus, they are the only one responsible.

Though a person reacting to their action cannot be blamed for choosing to counterstrike, all reaction does is set the two up for a new set of battles. Thus, though the original instigator holds all the karma, the battles may be never ending.

So, here we are in the world of #metoo and #timesup. There were two people seeing life the way they see it. Two people doing what they do, defined by how they learned how to behave in the position they find themselves in life. And thus, from doing what they do, they have either hurt someone, helped someone, or find themselves on the receiving end of negativity and hating the person or persons who put them on that receiving end.

Two people. Two stories. Two sets of life experiences. Two sets of excuses for why they did what they did.

There are always two sides of the story and the truth lies somewhere in the middle or is there? One person did something to the other person that they did not want to happen to them. Though they may have been forced into a life-situation where they had to give into it happening to them, that does not make it right. If you hurt someone, you are at fault. If you make somebody do something they did not want to do, you are at fault. If you helped somebody you are also at fault. But, which fault do you think is more appropriate?

Start defining your life by questioning, *"What is what I'm about to do going to do to the life of someone else and what will what I do ultimately mean to my life?"*

* * *
06/Feb/2018 07:01 AM

There is only so much fight you can put into what someone else says or does.

* * *

06/Feb/2018 06:55 AM

Give.

* * *
06/Feb/2018 06:55 AM

Can you ever be anything else?

* * *
06/Feb/2018 06:50 AM

If the only person you have to talk to is god then you are out of touch with life.

*   *   *
06/Feb/2018 06:49 AM

You've said something, you've done something that negativity affected another person. If you don't care about the impact that you've had on that person you are not worthy of relevance.

* * *
06/Feb/2018 06:49 AM

Not knowing is also a sin.

* * *
05/Feb/2018 06:43 AM

Take today and do good things.

If you see someone that needs help, help them.

If you see or hear someone doing something bad or saying something negative, tell them to stop.

If you have done something wrong that has hurt someone or said something that negativity affected their life, do all that you can to correct it.

Take today and care more about the everybody else than yourself.

The Ghost of Christmas Future
04/Feb/2018 07:20 AM

Sometimes, in the afternoon, if I have a moment, I like to take what was deemed in the 1980s, a Power Walk. Though I have always been a brisk walker, so I am not doing anything different, but it provides me with a little time to separate my mind from whatever I am working on or thinking about, walk around the neighborhood, and get in a little bit of exercise.

Yesterday, my lady and I had set out. We were walking up this one street when up ahead, this elderly man comes running around the corner. It is important that I describe him as this sets the whole story in motion. I would guess him to be in his eighties. He obviously had experienced a stroke. He was learning noticeably to one side and was running with his paces very close together. His movements were very animated. And, his short stride kept him from making very much forward progress. It was really kind of sad to watch. I guess it was his wife who followed him very closely behind. She was literally yelling at him to show down. The man would hear none of it. Obliviously, in his mind, he was still a young vibrant specimen and he was out for a run. He kept going up the hill a bit and BAM he fell down. Fell down hard.

As a martial artists, I have witness this style of behavior quite often with long-time practitioners who forget their age, do not adapt, and attempt to perform their techniques as if they were still in their twenties. But, they are not. In your late teens or twenties your body is fluid. By your thirties your body begins to show obvious signs of deterioration. By your forties and fifties one's body is substantially less agile and is much more prone to injury but many people forget this fact and attempt to behave as if they are still young. But, they are not.

It's the same when you are out in the out and about. You can watch as older men (and sometimes older women) try to hit on people who are substantially younger than themselves when the younger person is not interested at all. This age inappropriate behavior just makes them look bad...

Barring any unforeseen circumstance, I will hit the age of sixty this year. Damn, that's old! ☺ And, though I feel pretty good, I know that my body is not what it once was. Thus, I try work within my own boundaries, definitions, and limitations.

The thing is, if we live long enough, we are all going to get there. We are all going to get old. When we do, (and really at every step along the way), it is essential that we respect our age and live defined by the boundaries of where we find ourselves in life.

Some people are very lucky, they make it into old age with the ability to remain very active. You see them on the news sometimes. That's great! Unfortunately, not everyone is like that. Some people get injured, some people get sick, some people have strokes, some people just get old. But, whatever the case, wherever you find yourself in life, we each have a Ghost of Christmas Future. How you behave in this moment, how you treat your body right now, and how you treat other people, will lead you to where you will find yourself when you get there. Do the right thing now and hopefully your tomorrow, when you are old, will be okay...

The World of Judgment
03/Feb/2018 12:54 PM

Many people live in a world of judgment. They judge everyone and everything. Some may say that they judge based upon the way that they were judged. Other would say that their judgment is based upon a sense of entitlement, arrogance, and all-knowingness. Wherever an individual's mindset of judgment comes from, what it sets into motion is a world where someone is right, someone is wrong, and personal expression and emancipation are not allowed.

As one travels through life, you can witness as a person gets older, whether or not their mind becomes more refined or more embedded with a sense of their own righteousness. In some cases, people who were once judgmental evolve and become more understanding of the fact that each individual operates from a perspective of their own state of mind and life understanding. In other cases, people simply become more and more harsh and more rooted in their sense of they know what is right, wrong; good or bad.

How a person views the world is the defining factor of all they will encounter in the world. How a person views and judges other people is what sets the process for their personal life evolution and advancement into motion.

From a perspective of refined consciousness, it is commonly understood that being judgmental is not only a detriment to one's self but to the overall expanding evolution of life, as well. For if one is living their life from a space of being judgmental, they are not only hindering the forward movement of interpersonal learning within themselves but they also hinder the expansion of knowledge to all those they encounter who listen to their evaluation of other people and other life situations that they provide.

So, where do you find yourself in life? Are you a person who immediately believes they know what they know before they ever allow a person or a situation to simply be who and/or what they are? Or, are you silent and take the time to understand that each person operates from their own level of understanding, based upon what they have been given in life, and from this allow each person to make their own unique contribution to life without the need to predicate that contribution upon the basis of whether or not you do or do not like it.

Your Interpretation of What You Hear
03/Feb/2018 05:04 AM

When you hear or read something do you interpret the words in a negative fashion or in a positive one? Do you seek something to dislike and become angry at or do you look for the good in what is presented as bad?

Everything you hear, everything you read is interpreted by you. How you listen, how you read and what you are looking for in what you hear and what you read is a clear definition of who you are as a person. If you hear or read words and you focus on the negative in what they illustrate, you are basing your life upon negativity. If on the other hand, you take what you hear or read and always look for the positive, you are basing your life on positivity.

Who you are is what you portray. Who you are is what causes you to unleash either negativity or positivity to the greater whole of the world. Who you are sets your destiny into motion. If it is negative, if what you spread is negativity, then though you may thrive in the internalization and emulation of that form of internal energy, eventually it will come to take its toll on you.

This is the same with being drawn to the positive. If that is what you seek, if that is what you surround yourself with, even though you may not be successful by worldly standards, your life is the embodiment of goodness. Thus, your positive destiny is clear.

People can choose to be negative or people can choose to be positive. No matter what factors influenced you or brought you to where you find yourself in life; who you are is ultimately your choice. How you interpret what you listen to, how you interpret what you read—what you write, what you say, and what you do is also your choice.

Who and what do you want to be? Someone who hurt the All and the Everything with negativity or someone who helps, all that you can, with positivity?

Negative is negative. Positive is positive. There is no in-between. If you hurt you hurt. If you help you help. Who will you choose to be?

What Happens to Those People?
02/Feb/2018 02:25 PM

I was driving down a main street yesterday and this guy drives straight through a stop sign from a side street and is heading right for me. Luckily, I react in time and swerve out of his way. Of course, I am angry, honking and screaming. I drive down the road a bit to turn into the driveway I was originally headed for and begin to turn in. The guy drives by me, honks, and flips me off. My initially reaction was that I put my car in reverse and thought to go and confront him and possibly kick his ass. But, I catch myself, knowing that road rage equals nothing good. So, I just let it go.

But, here's the thing, I did nothing wrong. Yet, here was this guy, who did do something wrong, and yet he is accosting me like it was my fault.

As you have passed through your life how many times has someone drawn you into a very negative situation that you did not ask for, did not want, and had nothing to do with creating?

In life, there are all kinds of levels of subtlety in interpersonal relationships. For example, when something goes bad in a relationship, in many cases, fault can be pointed to in several directions. But, that is interpersonal stuff. That's not the point of this piece. I'm talking about the bigger scale of life, when someone you do not know drags you into melodrama. In these cases, there is commonly one person at fault. That person is the individual who instigate the ongoing play of events.

Now, this can be a random act like what occurred to me yesterday. I'm sure the guy didn't set out to almost hit my car but, via unconscious action, he almost did. This is the same case with most accidents. But, then there is the other side of the picture when somebody consciously sets about doing something to someone else. Maybe they steal something from someone. Maybe they physically hurt them. Maybe they tell them a lie which causes them to make an inappropriate choice or decision which leads to other negative events in their life farther down the line. Maybe they say something negative about a person that is then broadcast to other people, which then causes negative occurrences to be brought to the life of the person they were speaking about. The list of possibilities is really endless…

    At the source point of truly negative action is one person doing one thing that sets a negative course of events into motion in the life of another person.

    Now, say for example that guy would have hit my car yesterday. I mean, people have run into my cars and motorcycles in the past. Yes, that probably would have caused a whole slew of negative events to occur in both of our lives. But, though it would have been his fault, he did not set out on a course to intentionally hurt someone else. Thus, his karma is negligible.

    On the other hand, a person who sets out and consciously steals, takes, hurts, says something, speaks a lie, falsely judges a person, spread negativity, or anything like that, they are directly responsible for their actions and the occurrences that result to the life of the other person because of what they did.

    Do you ever question your actions before you do what you do? Do you ever think about what will happen to the other person because of you doing what you are about to do?

I think one of the most interesting things at the root of at this very common level of human behavior is the fact that the, *"Doer,"* always denies or justify their responsibility. They try to talk their way out of the fact that they did something wrong that hurt the life of someone else. They try to find reason, logic, and justification for having done what they did. But, the truth is, they hurt someone else. They hurt them by choosing to do something. Maybe they were spurred along by family or friend. Maybe it was just a self-conceived action. Maybe it was just a random selfish act. But, once it was done—once they were called out for doing it, they spend an enormous amount of time and energy justifying what they have done. Why can't they just say, *"Sorry. Let me try to fix what I have broken."* But no, that is rarely the case.

So, back to the original/title question… What happens to those people? I don't know? I guess it is different for each case. In my life, I have watched as some ended up in jail, some have ended up broke and broken, while other have just continued along. Many, I intentionally lost touch with so I have no idea what happened to them. But, the fact is, they took, they stole, they hurt, they lied, they spoke; equaling damage to another person's life. So ultimately, whenever they get what they get for doing what they did, they will be paid back. End of story.

If you have hurt someone, you are wrong. If you have consciously tried to hurt someone through theft, violence, or words, you are very-wrong. If you have hurt someone by not caring enough to take them into consideration before you did what you did, you are wrong. Wake up and try to undo what you have done. Care enough about the humanity of the, *"Someone else,"* to do something that makes a positive difference in their life. Do not always think only about yourself.

The Different Textures of Pasta
02/Feb/2018 07:12 AM

I was going to cook up a meal based on pasta last night and I was astounded to hear a person tell me that all pasta tastes the same—all the various shapes and sizes. This made me smile in disbelief and realize how people never study the various textures of life and how those textures affect everything.

Pastas are all very different. This is not just to detail the obvious difference between the traditional, the whole wheat, the enriched, and the etc... But, how it is made, the subtitles of the ingredients used in its creation, and the shapes all play a part in how pasta tastes.

It can be argued that the sauce is the true defining factor of any pasta dish. But, do you ever eat pasta without sauce. I do that most of the time. I just use butter. It's great! Try it.

But the shape and texture of the pasta also really defines the taste of the pasta. Its texture really adds to the overall experience.

There are a whole lot of shapes and sizes and names of pasta. Whether it is the traditional spaghetti, fettuccini, penne, rotini, rigatoni, of vermicelli; I mean the list is really-really long. If you feel like it, search pasta on the inter-web and you will see just how many shapes and sizes there are. A lot...

Yes, all of these shapes, sizes, and styles, may have a similar ingredient based origin; based upon the company who created it, (or if you personally create pasta at home), but the reason for the different shapes and sizes is all based on the flavor they will present in the meal.

Weird, I know… But, really… Do you ever take the time to actually taste your food? Do you take the time to study the subtitles? If you don't, you are really missing out.

This life is all you have. Taste it.

The Guy Who Never Made a Movie
The Guy Who Never Wrote a Book
01/Feb/2018 07:05 AM

  I find it rather interesting/amusing that every now and then someone will heads-up me to the fact that this one guy is out there attempting to cast shade on me as a filmmaker—criticizing my films and/or me in one derogatory way or the other. The funny thing is, and the thing that anybody who reads his posts does not realize, is that it was like ten years ago or so the guy first contacted me directly saying something negative and telling me he could and has made a better movie than I ever could. I gave him my address and told him to send me a copy. Of course, he never did, as he has never made a film. Yet, there he is, still out there, throwing around negativity focused at me and I imagine other people, as well. But, who is he really angry at? Me for making movies or himself for never making one?

  Maybe twenty years, when my first book on Hapkido came out, I was contacted by this school owner telling me how terrible the book was. I suggested that he write one. He told me, of course he would, and it would be so much better than mine. Great, I told him, I look forward to reading it. But, that book was never created. I guess he either never wrote the book or he found out how impossible it is to actually get a deal with an established publishing company. All these years later, still no book on Hapkido from him…

  You know, when I first began putting the formalized foundations for Zen Filmmaking together; the words I spoke, the classes I taught, and the writing that were published were all designed to help the person who may be having a problem getting his or her film actually done. The teachings were put together as an inspiration. This is still the case. But, back then, all the so-called, know-it-all, wanta-be filmmakers were saying Zen Filmmaking was all wrong. A film could never be made without a script. But, that was never the point. The point was, JUST DO IT! Simplify and get it done! Since that time, I have still received the same words of criticism. Sure, there are a lot of people who have made a lot of indie films since I first came up with Zen Filmmaking almost thirty years ago. But, there are also a lot more who have failed. ...Failed for whatever reason. Mostly, as I have said so many times, the reason people fail in their filmmaking process is their expectations. They want their movie to look like a several million-dollar production when all they have is a few hundred dollars. Or, they wait and wait, hoping the big bank will come their direction but it never does. But, if you let go of your expectation, if you let go and allow yourself to be free in your vision, you can actually get something done. You can actually make a movie or create anything else that you want to create.

This is the same with all things in life. Maybe you have a vision. Maybe you even dislike what someone else has created and want to do it better. But, until you have shown what you can actually do it and put it on the same chopping block of public opinion—exposing it to the same damnation, then all you are is voice speaking words that holds no true validly.

Maybe you don't want to make a movie. Maybe you don't want to write a book. And, that's great. That's who you are. But, if you do, then do it. Sitting around telling someone else/everyone else how bad they are, how bad what they are doing is, means you are doing nothing.

Once in a Blue Moon
31/Jan/2018 08:05 AM

There's the old saying, *"Once in a blue moon,"* meaning it happens very rarely. What is a, *"Blue Moon?"* The second full moon in a single month. Though they are not all that rare, they don't happen all the time. In fact, one happened last night. Did you know that? And, do you care?

How many blue moons have occurred throughout your lifetime? Have you taken note of each? Have you taken note of any? How many other unique stellar experiences have occurred? Did you even know that they occurred and if you did, did you care?

The majority of most people lives is defined solely by what they personally care about: what is going on in their life, how they feel, and who they feel what about. Everything else is just mind junk. They never take note of any passing events. Though this is the commonality defining the life of most people, so much of life is lost by not taking note of the ongoing occurrences throughout the span of your existence—as your interactive experiences, throughout your life, is all that you have that defines your existence.

Sure, we may not be all that interested in certain things. But, that does not mean that we should not experience them to the best of our ability, wherever we find ourselves in life. For if we don't, all we are left with is a life lived defined solely by what was trapped in our brain, defined by whatever level of emotion we were experiences at that point in time.

Reach out. Expand. Experience.

* * *
30/Jan/2018 05:32 PM

You can make a choice.

You Will Be Photographed
29/Jan/2018 06:52 AM

Taking pictures of family and friends has been the norm forever. But, since the dawning of the digital age, and everyone having a camera with them all the time, taking pictures of unknown people has also become quite common.

I think having our picture taken by someone we don't know pisses most of us off. I know it does me. ...I mean unless you are some sort of glory hound or fame whore or something, you really don't want your picture taken by some unknown stranger. But, it seems that everywhere we go now, there is some person taking photos with their smartphone or videotaping an entire scene from their selfie stick. For the most part, I guess, this is pretty harmless. But, that doesn't mean that most of us want our image being captured for who knows what purpose???

Having traveled the world for much of my adult life, I know I have been a photographic sinner, as well. I have taken photos of a lot of people across the globe. In most cases, out of respect, I make sure that the person knows and accepts the fact that I am taking their photo. But, I too have done a certain amount of long lens image captures.

I totally get it when some celebrity freaks out at a photographer who is taking their picture when they do not want it taken. I mean, here in L.A. there are paparazzi all over the place. It is one thing when some random stranger is just trying to let his family and friends know where he was and what he has seen, but it is a whole other issue when a guy with a $5,000.00 camera is getting up in your business.

I think back to the first time I was about to go off on a guy taking my picture. I was in this Italian restaurant, in San Francisco, a couple of decades back and my lady noticed this guy was sitting at a table on the other side of the restaurant, taking our photos. I got up and was about to go off but he saw me coming, knew what I was upset about, and said he would immediately delete the photos. *"Here look, I just got rid of them."* AOK. He was just a photo geek trying to capture some art with his first-generation digital camera.

I was at the 2018 NAMM Show over the past few days. This is a big music industry event, where they showcase all the new equipment, that attracts a lot of music celebrities. I was walking into one of the rooms and this guy with a high-end Canon DSLR camera grabs a shot of my lady and me. I immediately glare at him and he scurries away. Did it piss me off? Yes, it did. Because the problem with the *paps* is, you never know what they're going to do with the photos. But, what could I do? Smash his camera and kick his ass?

This is just the reality of the today; your photo is going to be taken. In fact, pretty much every business you go into, every venue or airport you walk through, and many of the city streets you walk along; you are being photographed.

I think back to my early emersion in the film industry. I had a role in this film and we were shooting at LAX. As it was a medium budget movie, they simply paid for the right to shoot outside one of the terminals but not to shut it down. They put up a big sign saying if you walk through this film set you may be on camera and you may be in a movie. Did the people who needed to travel from one terminal to the next or make their way to their car or taxi have a choice? No, not really. But, interesting approach, I thought. I wonder whatever happened to that movie?

As a Zen Filmmaker, I have shot footage at a lot of public events and used it in films. Is that illegal? Absolutely not. The fact is, once you are in public, you are public. If someone is filming, they can film you and there is nothing you can do about it. That's how shows like TMZ, Cops, and Live PD get away with it. In fact, (kinda funny) back when they were filming Extra at The Grove and they were interviewing Arnold, I was walking through and it was like one of those strange conditions but almost as if it was orchestrated, in every cut they did, there I was passing by in the background. ☺

So, here we are… Here in the digital age… Do most of us want to be photographed at every juncture of our existence? No, but there is not a damn thing we can do about it. You will be photographed.

*   *   *

28/Jan/2018 07:47 AM

A lot of people say a lot of things.

People are always happy to voice their opinion.

But, what are you actually doing to help the people who need help and make the world a better, more positive place?

Friends: Sorta, Maybe, Kinda
27/Jan/2018 05:26 PM

What kind of a friend are you? Do you support someone you like when they are behaving the way you want them to behave? Do you support someone you like when they do something that you do not like? Do you stand up for them, to other people, when someone says something mean or negative about them? Are you willing to step up and go face-to-face, toe-to-toe when someone is threatening them?

Most friendships are lost in the condition of doing business. When a person is happy with the way a person is behaving they are friends. The moment someone does something they do not like; the friendship is over. But, this is not true friendship at all. This is just doing business. It is an exchange of niceties. Friendship is much more than that. True friendship is accepting the good with the bad—enjoying the nice times but being willing to stand up for and forgive someone when they do something that you do not like.

Take a look at your so-called friendships. How deep are they? How long have the lasted? Have they been there for you through thick and thin; the good and the bad? Have they remained your friend when you did something that they did not like? Now, flip the coin, have you remained their friend when they did something that you did not like?

Most friendships are Goodtime Charlie friendships. People remain friends while things are good. But, the moment they are not good, *"Goodbye."*

But, more than simply taking the good with the bad and forgiving when a wrong is said or done; do you stand up for your friends? Do you take other people to task if they are saying something negative about your friend? Do you do this even though it may bring condemnation your direction? Do you stand up for them even if they do not know you are taking that action? Do you do it when there is no reward offered for your actions?

Most people do not do this. Most people will not stand up for their friends. Most people are not willing to go to battle for their friendships. Thus, and again, most friendships are not true friendships at all.

Take a few moments and think about the friendships you have had throughout your life. Think about how your friends have behaved towards you and how you have behaved towards your friends. Were they a true friend to you and were you a true friend to them?

True friendships begin with you: how you treat a person, how you act around a person, and how you defend a person. As friendships begin with you, how you treat your friends will be how your friends will treat you.

Think about who you are. Are you willing to be a true friend?

The Price That Was Paid
27/Jan/2018 07:02 AM

Do you ever take the time to ponder what price was paid by a particular individual to get to the place that they got to in life? Do you ever question what that person went through to arrive at the position where you find them at in their life?

Think about your own life. Think about where you find yourself in life. What did it take for you to arrive at the position where you now discover yourself? Whether you love or hate where you are right now in your life, you did not get there by accident. There was destiny you encountered, choices you made, actions you took, people you interacted with, things you did, words you spoke, that all equal where you find yourself today.

Was your life easy? Where you surround by supportive and encouraging people that helped you along your way? Or, did you have to fight your way through life, motivated only by yourself, to achieve anything that you have achieved? Whatever the case, your life is your life. As this is your life, this is where many people stop their pondering. They lock themselves into their own mind: their advancements, their feelings, their emotions, their trial and their tribulations. They think only about themselves. They do this, though they interact with other people on a daily basis. They take things from other people. They expect things from other people. Yet, they never ponder how and why a person has come to the place they are in life, where they have anything to offer them at all.

Each of our lives is a unique blend of happenstance and chosen direction. Each of our lives is defined by what we were given and what we personally achieved. No one is whole and completely created by themselves. They have been given things by other people, they have been taught by other people, some have even stolen from other people. But, the fact is, no one does not owe someone something.

So, back to the original question(s)... Do you ever take the time to ponder what price was paid by a particular individual to get to the place that they got to in life? Do you ever question what that person went through to arrive at the position where you find them at in their life?

Every person that you interact with in your life, you owe something. This is especially the case if they are in a position where they formally give you something: be in help, kindness, love, education, or your wages. If you do not take the time to come to understand how they got to the position where they have arrived, you are a selfish person who is lost in a world of only thinking about yourself and what you can take from someone else. Be more. Come to understand that each person has paid a price to arrive at the position where they have arrived at in life. If you can understand the cost they paid you can understand that everyone deserves respect.

* * *
26/Jan/2018 02:06 PM

Hurting the one who has hurt you only causes more hurt.

Where does the hurting end?

*   *   *

26/Jan/2018 01:33 PM

As long as the hurt you instigated still hurts, you cannot be forgiven.

The Court of Public Opinion
26/Jan/2018 09:40 AM

Recently, there has an outpouring of accusation throughout the entertainment industry. With the rapid birth of the #metoo and the #timesup movement, many people have voiced their outrage at what has been taking place. (I too wrote a blog about what has happened to me awhile back). This is obviously a good thing. Every now and then there is a social outcry and from these movements, society changes.

Just as in life, change needs a motivating factor. But, the fact is, at the personal level, most people never change. They fall into a pattern of behavior and they remain in that mindset throughout their life. Whether this is a positive frame of mind or a negative one, that is who and what they are and what they emulate. Commonly, the only time interpersonal change ever occurs, in most people, is when it is forced down their throat. Maybe this is caused by the injury or the death of a loved one or by being told they only have a few days or a few weeks left to live. But, without this forced motivation, nothing is ever altered.

Though forced change, especially on the larger scale, can be a very good thing for society, there is also a downside to this. This downside is that of, *"Accusation."* Though an accusation may or may not be true, once it is spoken it has the potential to truly damage a person's life.

Have you ever had someone make a false accusation about you? If you have, then you understand the damage that can be inflicted to your life. Though you can scream at the top of your lungs, *"That's not true,"* some people will still believe it. Thus, your life will be altered forever simply by what one person said.

I could go into all the negative karma repercussions about doing something like that. But, this is not something the person unleashing the words thinks about. They dislike a person, for any number of reasons, and from this, they want to hurt them. So, no matter what you say to them, they will do what they do without the care for the consequences to the person they are speaking about or the later consequences to themselves.

Yesterday, I was at The NAMM Show. As I was standing in the long line to go through the security checkpoint, a man in line with me began a conversation. He began by stating that, *"I guess we need to go through this to be safe."* He continued on to discuss all of the latest acts of terror—including the recent one involving a teenager shooting up his classroom. He stated, *"Everyone is so angry now."* This is a very true point. There is a lot of anger in the world right now. This anger is motivated by any number of things. In the entertainment industry, it is most notably motivated by the false promise of ongoing fame and fortune that many of the people, throwing the accusations, have not achieved. They focus their attention on those who are winning the awards or are at the top of the game. ...For who cares about anyone at the bottom of the ladder? Saying something about them will cause no new notoriety to be focused on those speaking out. But, speaking about those at the top will cause new attention to be drawn to the accusers. And, of course, for the great motivator for the everything of everything; money. Give me some of yours!

Now, this is a difficult subject, because a lot of people are angry. From this, the moment you offer them up a new person to be angry at, there is a frenzy.

The fact is, the only two people who know the truth about anything that went on between them are those two people. And, many times, there are two very different points of view. This is not necessarily right or wrong but it is the way it is.

I am not saying that a forcible anything is right. And, a person who forcibly hurts, injures, steals, slanders, and all of that stuff, should be held accountable for their actions. But, before you can cast any blame you need to know the facts and not simply the facts presented by one person attempting to gain notoriety by what they are saying. Remember, if you say something about anybody else, you are the one gaining notice by mentioning their name—not only does this invoke all kinds of levels of karma but in the end, all you are defining yourself as is someone who is defined by that other person and any relationship you did or did not have thereof.

Ask yourself, *"Have you ever been hurt by anybody?"* Now, ask yourself, *"Have you ever hurt anybody?"* I believe that most of us will answer, *"Yes,"* to both of those questions.

The ultimate definitions of these answers are, however, defined by individual perspective. This is not right or wrong, this is just the way it is.

So, before you believe anything about anybody, that you do not have personal knowledge about, ask yourself, *"Why are you believing it,"* and then question, *"How is your own interpersonal level of unresolved anger motivating your belief?"*

In life, everything comes down to you: all you think, all you speak, and all you believe.

We each have been hurt by other people. We each have hurt other people. It is what we do with these facts that defines us as human beings. For those who have hurt us, it is the ultimate sacrifice to forgive them. Thus, freeing us from any further karma. For those we have hurt, it is the ultimate step forward to grow as a human being and become better people so we will hurt no one else. We need to fix what we can to those we have wronged and help the world become a better place through love: not anger, not accusations.

* * *
25/Jan/2018 06:52 AM

Does a good person do bad things or do bad people simply pretend to be good?

* * *
25/Jan/2018 06:50 AM

You can take any fact and make it sound positive or negative by the way it is presented. Thus, though facts may be factual, they are defined by personal interpretation.

* * *
24/Jan/2018 04:50 PM

Who are you to claim that you know anything about anything?

You should ask yourself this question before you ever speak because someday you may have to provide an answer to this question to someone who actually matters.

* * *

24/Jan/2018 04:49 PM

Some people spend their entire life making up for what they have done wrong.

Do you even care about what you've done wrong?

* * *

24/Jan/2018 11:37 AM

The pain you have caused someone else is the ultimate definition of your life.

The sooner you realize this, the sooner you can begin to undoing the pain you have caused and lessen any further pain you will inflict.

How Long is Long Enough?
24/Jan/2018 11:31 AM

When you live in Shangri-La, you are young and beautiful forever.

When you leave Shangri-La, you immediately become old and grey.

Life is lived by the perception of time. When you are young, time is seemingly endless. There will always be enough of it to make what you want happen. There is always tomorrow. The longer you live life, the more time passes. This infiniteness of time becomes quite finite, however.

When you are young, you dismiss age. You dismiss the aged.

As you get older, you see the folly of this pervious understanding.

When you are twenty, you see fifty or sixty as very old. *"That's thirty or forty years from now! That's plenty of time to live."* But, when you reach forty, the countdown clock begins and you realize a new perspective on life and on time.

Do you know someone who has died at a young age due to what they did to themselves? Maybe this was drugs. Drugs are bad! Sure, they make you feel good, but they kill so many people, so young. Maybe this was alcohol. Think how many people have killed themselves via alcohol related illness and how many people have been killed by the drink driver—not to mention how many fights have erupted due to alcohol intoxication where people's entire lives have been changed due to that altercation. Maybe it was cigarettes. When I see someone smoking, I tell them about the fact that I knew someone who died from lung cancer at the age of thirty-two. But, they all dismiss this statement, believing it will never happen to them. But, think about how many nonsmoker's lungs, lives, and health the smoker has invaded via their secondhand smoke. I've known others who died from lung cancer in their late fifties or early sixties. Not to mention how many people I have witnessed their skin age prematurely, become old before their time, and incurring heart attacks and other health issues due to smoking. But, the young have forever... Age and death will never happen to them. Sixty is old. *"If I can live another thirty years, I'll be happy,"* they exclaim. But, will you? Will that be enough? What about when you get there—if you get there? Then, what? When you are at the gates of death, how will you feel? Will you feel the time you had was enough—that you got to love the people you love long enough—that they will be okay without you?

Youth is Shangri-La. Shangri-La is the deception of life. But, time catches up with everyone. Thus, how you live your time and what you do to yourself and to others while you are living your time is all you will have when you are in the last moments of your life. Think about what you are during now that is ultimately equally your final moments in life.

* * *
23/Jan/2018 06:58 AM

Unseen is unknown.

* * *
23/Jan/2018 06:57 AM

Why do people cry in the presence of holiness?

Because they are ashamed of their sins.

*   *   *
23/Jan/2018 06:53 AM

If your anger rises and you feel exhilarated because someone is saying something negative about another person, that in and of itself should be a warning to you that the person you are listening to is one of the source points for the negative energy that is permeating this world and making life less livable.

Moving Very Fast to Stand Still
22/Jan/2018 07:36 AM

Do you feel you are accomplishing what you what to achieve in your life?

Some people do.

Some people don't.

Some people do not think about this subject at all.

In life, some people are provided with the opportunity to chart an abstract course towards an achievement they desire. They are allowed to do this because: one, they have the formalized desire to achieve a focused end-goal and two, they have been provided with the opportunity to be financially secure enough to have the time to dream in the first place.

Look around the world, most people are trapped into an existence of survival. They must do what they do, each and every day, simply to be able to have enough to eat. Joy and the desire to achieve their dreams are all but removed from their life. All that exists in their mind is finding a way to subsist.

The people in the modern world—the people who read this blog are, for the most part, not like this, however. They live in a space of relative freedom where the achievement of dreams are possible and are, in fact, suggested and promised. But, do most people walk down a road towards the achievement of their dreams? Or, do they remain trapped in the mundane?

All (personal) dream have a price tag attached to their achievement. That price tag may be paid by the dreamer themselves. That price tag may be paid by others. That price tag may destroy the dream and the dreamer. But, if the price is not paid, no dreams are livable. This is the conundrum of existence in the free world. Dreams are promised. The dreams lived by others are broadcast. But, the pursuit of dreams can mean the destruction of all a person ever had and/or could become.

Do you know a person who works day-in and day-out at a job they do not like? Why do they do that? Survival.

If you are lucky enough to not have to ponder your day-to-day survival you are blessed. But, what do you do with that blessing? Most people who are blessed exist in a space of arrogance. Because they don't have to worry about the reality of where they will live, what they will eat, they are removed from the truth of existence. Thus, all they know is not based upon realized knowledge, it is simply based upon privilege. And, this is where all of the problems of the world begin. This is where the dreamers damn themselves to living a life defined by negative karma. As they are not existing at the root of life itself, they are making their way through their existence via the creations, the thoughts, the works, and the toil of others.

As you pass through your life, how much time do you spend studying and/or caring about what has caused you to maintain your existence at the space where you find yourself? Do you ever reach out and thank and perhaps pay-back the people who have allowed you to rise to and to exist at your current state of being? ...The ones you love and those you hate... For both of them are responsible for you being where you are. Do you even think of who is responsible for you being where you are and who you are? Do you acknowledge the person or persons who has provided you with the ability to dream?

Your dreams are your dreams. Your desires are your desires. Your life is your life. Where has it been? Where is it going? Why are you where you are on your path towards achievement? And, who is ultimately responsible for you being there?

Here is the list of questions that you must ponder as your embark on a path towards achieving your dream:

Are you walking in place or are you consciously walking forward?

Who are you walking on and who are you walking over to get to what you are attempting to become?

What are you planning to give back if and when you reach your life's dream?

And finally, what if you never reach your desired dream? What will your life have meant as you pursued your dream walking through your existence?

* * *
21/Jan/2018 08:12 AM

What if you could only do one thing one time?

What would you do before you did it?

The Something That You Never Got
21/Jan/2018 08:00 AM

For virtually all of us, there is something that we wanted in our life that we never received. Maybe this was something small or maybe it was something large. Yet, by not receiving it, we have never forgotten the wanting.

For some, that something occurred in childhood—something that we truly believed we needed. As a child, our finances are limited. Thus, and as such, we commonly do not have the money to buy it for ourselves. As we could not obtain it, in some cases, these things haunt our entire life.

I think to one woman I know. Her family immigrated to the United States. As such, her parents were not well educated in American culture. Valentine's Day came around. For those of us from The States, (and perhaps some of those from other countries), we understand that it is common tradition to pass out Valentine's Day cards to all of our young classmates. The box of them only cost a dollar or two. But, her parents refused to buy them for her. Thus, she stayed up all night, the night before Valentine's Day, making cards out of paper and crayons. For her, this was humiliating and totally devastating. Something she has never forgotten. Even for me, knowing the importance of this tradition, every time I think of it, I become very sad. It makes me want to cry.

Such a small thing. But, something that comes to define a life.

For each of, in our childhood, we probably have moments like this. Perhaps not so life-shaping, but moment defined by what we knew we needed and did not have.

Adolescence is no different. I know my early adolescence was horrible. Totally defined by what I did not have. The thing was, I could have had it, as we were not poor. But, my mother never saw beyond her own realm of self-definition and needs, so she did not see what the not having was doing to her son. For me, looking back at that period, all I can see is the shame and the feeling of need.

Again, we all have these moments. For some it is less, for others is it more. But, they are all defined by how what we did not have comes to define us as people. It causes us to act and react; to live our life defined upon these factors.

Many adults want many things. As adults, they have many more resources available to obtain said desires. But, by obtaining them, it has driven many an adult into financial distress, bankruptcy, and even suicide.

People also want other people. They want them to be theirs. But, here lies one of the most complicated areas of desire. As people are who they are, they each want what they want, and what they want may have nothing to do with another person who wants them. Thus, the person wanting one specific person may be totally left out in the cold when it comes to the desire fulfillment of another person. A lot of people have lived an empty life because of desiring to be with one specific person. Or worse...

In Eastern Mysticism, the human condition of desire is always taught to be avoided. And, there is good reason for this. It leads to a lot of problems. If you have no desire, you are free. But, this ideology is virtually impossible to instigate—unless you are a monk. So, what does this leave us with? It leaves us with the fact that virtually all of us have points in our life highly defied by what we did not have. For most of us, we just move on. We live life the best we can, remembering those times but not allowing them to dominate who we ultimately become. For here arise one of the key problems to living a good, psychologically healthy, and fruitful life; some people/many people become so defined by the moment(s) that they did not have what they felt they needed that the rest of their entire life comes to be defined by those moments causing them to act in a less than ideal manner and do bad/hurtful things throughout their entire existence. It becomes their excuse. It becomes their logic. I did not have this, so I do that. That is to say, it becomes their excuse if they are even mentally capable enough to be able to study their own mind and understand why they do what they do.

So, it ultimately comes down to this… There have been points in virtually all of our lives where we did not get what we needed/what we wanted. And, because of this, it truly changed our method of viewing and reacting to the world. But, we have to be aware enough that we control our minds, realizing that these moments cannot be allowed to become the defining factor of who we are and how we behave towards other people and the world as a whole. We <u>must</u> create ourselves.

So, the next time you see yourself feeling something negative or doing something negative, look back to its source point; seek it, find it, and do not allow it to control you. For if you want the world to be the positive world you create, you must be in control of yourself, hurt no one and make all things better. Never allow yourself to be defined by the what you never got.

Life Is Free. Or Is It?
19/Jan/2018 11:38 AM

I went to have breakfast at one of my usual haunts this morning. I went inside, ordered, filled up my cup of coffee, and went back outside to sit at a table. …I always sit outside whenever I can.

Sitting out there was this young attractive woman. She was on her laptop using the free Wi-Fi the restaurant offers and talking to someone over her internet phone. Sounded like she was running some sort of catering business. I noticed she hadn't ordered anything from the restaurant but I figured she just had some business to take care of first.

In any case, my breakfast arrived, I proceeded to eat it, and just as I was finishing up, the young woman ended her phone call. She closed her computer, got up, and went inside. I assumed it was to place her order. Anyway, with my breakfast completed, I got up to bring my plate inside. There, I notice that the young woman was leaving the bathroom. After that, she walked up to the coffee bar with her own travel mug, filled it up, and then she walked out the door. She didn't order anything. So… Here's the story, she came to the restaurant, used their free Wi-Fi, used their bathroom, got a free cup of coffee, and left. This made me smile.

Now, some people would see this as an interesting and inventive way to save money. And, I guess it is. I mean, she got everything for free. But, there is a whole other issue to this subject. An issue that very few people take the time to study—especially when they are taking a free ride. That issue is, if you base your existence upon taking things from people that they have not willingly given you, these actions will come to destroy your existence. Have you ever taken the time to study the life of someone who basis their income or their life upon taking? That taking can be large or it can be small but taking, by its very definition, is taking. By taking, you have gotten something for free that was not willingly given to you. Thus, the person you are taking from never made the agreement to give you that something. As all of life is based upon a conscious interaction of give and take—pay and receive, thus when someone finds the loophole and simply takes, all kinds of crazy energy is given birth to. Again, look at the lives of those who have based their existence upon taking; what becomes of them? The answer is, it never ends well.

This is an important thing to keep in mind as you pass through life. Sure, you can cheat the system and get things for free. Sure, you can cheat people and take things that they did not willing give you for free. But, at the end of the day, there is always a payment required. That is just the nature of human existence. So, taking for free is never free. There will always be a price to pay—if not today, someday…

The Value of What You Say
18/Jan/2018 08:48 AM

In the academic world, at the graduate level, to receive your degree you are required to write a thesis or a dissertation that is an original piece of work. Meaning, the focus of that research is never to have been done before. I think this is a great ideology in that from this organic research new levels of human understanding are attempted to be instigated.

As the modern age of the internet and self-publishing has come upon, it has given birth to people saying a lot of things about nothing. In many cases, these people present what they are saying as some form of original, revelation-based research but mostly it is just someone spitting out what they believe and they want others to believe. But, why? What is the basis for this brand of logic leading to proclaimed knowledge? What does it provide to the world?

The fact is, most people never even ponder this subject before they begin to expound their so-called wisdom. And, here lies the problem with the world as it currently stands; i.e. whom do you believe?

In the academic world, before you can write your thesis, you must develop a proposal and then present it to you graduate committee. They will read it, decide if they feel the study has merit, and then they may or may not approve it. The student may have to go back to the drawing board before they find a subject of research that will be approved. Once this occurs, the student must then study all of the previous research on the subject, write their original thesis, and then present and defend their paper to their graduate committee. Again, they may be sent back to the drawing board at any stage of this process. In fact, some never can finalize their research. But, this is all a good thing. It is a process of checks and balances providing a basis of and for approved factuality. What the people who have followed this path can say is that their area of study has been awarded factual merit. Thus, their degree.

Not everyone is suited to follow through to advanced levels of education. But, what each person should be able to cogitatively realize is the importance of accurate research before ever developing and broadcasting an opinion (disguised as fact) to the world. We should each, have the mental fortitude to be whole enough onto ourselves that we do not allow ourselves to be dominated by opinion to the degree where we come to believe it to be fact. Moreover, we should rebuke the people who live their life dominated by spreading their opinions outwards as they are the ones who are polluting the mind-space of humanity disguising belief as fact.

How many people do you know, who are the embodiment of positivity, that are dominated by being opinionated and broadcasting their opinions to the world? None, I believe. The people who base their life upon positivity do not need that kind of emotional stimuli. It is the people who are seeking outward approval based upon whatever engrained psychological demons they hold that they need to spread their opinions to the world.

It is essential to understand that simply because a person has a smile on their face that does not mean what they are saying to you is good, right, and/or factual.

So, where does this leave us? Where this leaves us is at the heart of the root of true understanding. Do you possess the ability to actual do the research and have your research approved by a wiser and knowing governing body before you feel you have something worth saying that should be heard by others? If you do, good for you. If you don't, think of all the karma you are creating for yourself by injuring people with your judgments disguised as knowledge.

*   *   *
18/Jan/2018 08:10 AM

When you don't know you don't know but why don't you know?

Partners in Crime and You Think You Know What You Never Know
17/Jan/2018 02:49 PM

As I have been discussing for many years now, some of the most influential martial arts practitioners of the twentieth century have all but been forgotten. Out of sight, out of mind, and all that… I think this is very sad as if you had the chance to meet them and perhaps train with them; they really had a lot to teach. But, unlike people like Bruce Lee, who wrote books and was seen in films, most of them never cast that large of a shadow. Thus, their knowledge was more secretive. Now, it is all but lost.

I have witnessed this to a degree with my Zen Filmmaking cohort, Donald G. Jackson, as well. Very few people knew him. Most who did, did not like him or he offended them. But, those who did pierce the veil and actually come to be friends with him understood that he was a unique and very creative individual. *"I'm an artist, god damn it,"* as he would joking exclaim. Together, we instigated Zen Filmmaking. Without his and my interaction, Zen Filmmaking would never have come to be. Certainly, there are those out there who may wish it would not have been created. ☺ But, with art at its heart, it was. From this, I have been allowed to formulate it into a relatively cohesive ideology and continue to follow the path he and I initiated, guiding the participant(s) towards cinematic enlightenment.

Once upon a time, people asked a lot of question about him. Now, zero… The only people who ever contact me, regarding him, are people that want to make money off of his movies by distributing them. No Thanks!

Sad, I think, he had a lot to say. Though, of course, he was completely self-centered, out of control, and crazy. But, he was a good friend and a visionary.

I have recently been contacted by a U.K. team that I am told is going to do a documentary on Zen Filmmaking. They didn't ask me if they could, they just decided to do it. ☺ They did ask me to do a little talk for it, however, but as I told them, I'm a fairly soft-spoken guy and I wouldn't want to bring down the intense energy of their production—as I have seen a trailer and it is great chaotic, psychedelic, anarchy. It sounds like they are going to use stuff from some other Zen Filmmakers out there. So, it will be interesting to see what they come up with and if they capture the essence of Zen Filmmaking or not.

In actually, I pretty much turn all requests for interviews down. Like I jokingly told my friend a number of years ago when we was giving me grief about turning down a TV spot, *"Hey, if it was Charlie Rose asking I would be there."* But now, sadly, even Charlie has fallen from grace.

A production team did do a big documentary about Zen Filmmaking and me in Hong Kong a number of years ago. I saw it in a theater over there. It was great. Big! Hong Kong style. But, it kind of went away. I don't really know what happened to it. I also lost track of the producers. So, it is in the wind somewhere. If you know where it is or have a copy, let me know.

But, this brings me to the point of all this… Back in the days when Don was still alive, it was so much more fun. It was fun to have a partner in crime. It was fun to not have to be the All and the Everything of every production. Though I certainly have worked with other filmmakers before and after Don, they all had agendas. They all wanted something other than the naturalness of Zen. They all had this idealized image of what a production should look like and what a finalized movie should be. A lot of the actors I have worked with totally got it and loved coming back for more. The so-called filmmakers, on the other hand, not so much. Thus, we all went our separate ways.

And, this is the thing about Zen Filmmaking, Donald G. Jackson, and Scott Shaw; what do you really know? Do you really know anything about me, him, or it? There are a few filmmakers out there who I am told I have influenced. Some large, some small. Some honest about their influences, some will never mention my name. In fact, maybe a month or so ago there was this guy who had obviously read my books and articles and his team had posted a doc about how he guides his actors with no script. He never mentioned Zen Filmmaking or me, but it was such an obvious rip off that it made me smile. But, that's okay, what can you do?

All you can do is do what you can do. That's what I do. I used to go at Zen Filmmaking with a much bigger scope of vision. But, as all that is left is me, (I have no partner in crime), I got tired of holding the weight of the All and the Everything on my shoulders. Thus, my vision became smaller, more abstract. Born was the Non-Narrative Zen Film. And, here's the thing about life; we all are here, we all are doing what we do, while wanting to do something else. But, what you are doing/what you can do is _all_ you can do. Do you create art in your moment as much as your moment will allow you? Or, do you let the immense gravity in the ALL of life keep you from doing anything?

Let's face it; creation is all any of us have. It is all that will be left when we leave this life. Whether your creations are loved or scorned, they are your creations. So, what are you going to create? What can you create alone when you don't have a partner in crime?

You Can't Put Your Mind into the Body of Another Person
17/Jan/2018 01:04 PM

You can't put your mind into the body of another person. You can't make them feel or act the way you would like them to act—the way you think they should behave.

It was kind of interesting/funny… I was in a store today. As I was walking by the men's shirts, I saw this middle-aged guy, shirtless, standing in the middle of the aisle, trying on various shirts with his big beer gut hanging out. My first impression was, *"How rude."* I mean, who would do that and why was store security letting him do that? I thought about the fact that I would be pissed if I bought a new shirt that had been on the sweaty body of that guy. Anyway, I walked on…

A bit latter, as I was leaving the store, this same guy was at the cash register. Loudly, he exclaimed, *"Are you shitting me? Fuck, you mean to tell me that this shirt is not on sale and some of your other one's are? Shit! Why did I waste my time trying this shirt on? Now I have to go back and look for something else. Fuck!"*

First of all, who talks like that to a person (the cashier) that they do not know? Plus, who loudly talks like that in public, while they are in line at a store? …There were other people in line.

I think for all of us thinking people, we would not even contemplate behaving in that manner. …The guy wasn't drunk or anything, he was just behaving the way he was behaving—the way he chooses to behave. Whatever brought him to that space in life where he talks like that with no regard or thought of others, I will never know but he was who he was and who he was, was a person who forces who he is onto others. Do you behave like that?

In life, most of us attempt to live in a space of refinement. We try to be better. We do not want to behave like the child having a tantrum. We want to be more than that. We do not want to force others to listen to our words. ...Words that some may find offensive. We do not want to damage the Life Space of any-one or any-thing.

Sadly, in life, this is not always the case, however. There are those who do not think of others or the affect they are having on others. They do what they do and they do not care. We can argue and debate the why of this equation forever. But, it will prove nothing. Some people are just loud, rude, and uncaring individuals. They say what they say because that is what they want to say and the rest of the world be damned. Sad, but true.

All we can do is be the best, most pure, most congenial, most helpful people we can be and never become like a person that makes a scene without ever even knowing they are making a scene. We should and can care about other people first. Like I always say, *"Be positive and smile."*

You can't put your mind into the body of another person. You can't make them feel or act the way you would like them to act—the way you think they should behave.

*   *   *

16/Jan/2018 04:36 PM

Your life is but a millisecond in the expansive span of eternity but every second of your life is all you have to live.

* * *

16/Jan/2018 04:35 PM

When you have done something that has hurt someone and what you did continues to hurt that person what does that do to the definition of your life and do you care?

* * *
16/Jan/2018 04:35 PM

You don't care about it until you care about it.

* * *

12/Jan/2018 11:55 AM

If someone forces you to do something against your will, they are one-hundred percent at fault.

If you choose to do something and later regret it, you are one-hundred percent at fault.

People should own their blame.

The Sound of Life
11/Jan/2018 10:15 AM

Do you take the time to listen to the sounds of life? Do you listen to all that is going on around you? No, not just the soothing and beautiful sounds of nature, but all of life. Even the sounds, the voices, the noises, and the music that you may not necessarily like.

We are each placed is a space of life. Where we find ourselves, in the overall evolution of history, is where we find ourselves. As we grow into adulthood we then may have the ability to move from one geographic environment to the next. In each new location, we will be confronted with new sounds. Each are the sounds of life.

As we progress through life, we are programmed into believing what sounds are nice and appropriate. We are taught which sounds to like. Then, with this as a basis, we decide what sounds to surround ourselves with. And, what sounds to repel. Some people may even attempt to make certain sounds stop. They may try to instigate methods that will countermand them. But, who and what are we to stop any of the sounds of life? Who and what are we to judge the sounds made by other people, other life forms, nature, and or the industrialize modern world. We may not like them but by attempting to rebuke them anything that we may learn from them is thereby lost.

So, ask yourself, do you listen to the sounds of life? Do you listen without judgment? Do you try to learn and gain experience from all that you hear? Or, do you simply try to block out what you do not find to be appropriate.

There are those who live life. There are those who experience life. Then, there are those who believe they already hold all of the answers and try to control life. Which one are you? And, at the end of your days, what will you have learned from what you did not allow yourself to hear?

The Peak Experience
10/Jan/2018 07:50 AM

Have you ever experienced one of those moments in life when all of a sudden everything just falls into place and you feel overwhelmingly great—all is well with your world? There are no real words to explain this emotion but it is simply an essential existential experience where everything is okay. From the tenets of New Age Philosophy this state of mind is known as, *"The Peak Experience."* It may most closely be linked to the ancient concept of *Satori* in Buddhism where a person encounters instantaneous enlightenment that may last but for a moment.

The concept of *The Peak Experience* was commonly talked about at the heyday of The New Age Revolution in the 1970s. In fact, it became a state of mind that people quested to encounter. Could it be found? Could it be encountered? Yes, of course it could. Like in all things in life, if you are looking for something it is much easier to find it than if you are not; i.e. you must know what you are looking for to care if you find and receive it.

The problem with a quest for a specific state of mind is that if and when it comes, it is defined by what you have heard and what you have read. Thus, lost is a naturalness of inner-revelation. It simply becomes an acknowledged state of consciousness that was promised.

If you have experienced this state of mind you will instantly attest to the fact that it feels pretty good. It is a state of All Being-ness. But, once it is experienced, then the re-experiencing of it is expected. When *The Peak Experience* remains absent, it is felt that something must be wrong with the mind of the individual. But, is it?

The problem is, with this state of mind, it will and can only be experienced when things are good in your life. The drawback with many a person's life is that their mind becomes bogged down with dealing with reality. There are bills to pay, desires to be achieved, and inner-personal conflicts to content with. Thus, a mind set up to actually encounter *The Peak Experience* is absent. Can this be remedied—even in this chaotic world? Sure. But, the <u>mind</u> within the <u>mind</u> must be found. A mind that can meet a state of mental grace even in admits the turmoil of everyday life. How do you do this? Silence your mind. But, here arises the problem. Do you care enough to silence your mind? Do you care about encountering the mental beauty of something that may only last a few seconds like a *Peak Experience?* Do you care about anything other than living, thinking, and being controlled by your day-to-day emotions, desires, and realities? Here lies the definition and the difference between someone who walks the Spiritual Path in order to encounter the Higher Mind and actually help all of humanity. It is all in the doing what you do and why you do it?

Today, the ideology of *The Peak Experience* has all but been forgotten. In some ways, this is not a bad thing as the person walking through the commonality of their life is not distracted by seeking the promised experience of the Higher Mind. But, there is also something lost in the fact that being reminded that the Higher Mind can be found by anyone—not just the monk liking in a monastery.

Satori is available. Enlightenment is available. *The Peak Experience* is available. Do you care?

* * *
10/Jan/2018 07:47 AM

If you do something that hurts someone you do not like, do you care?

If you don't, you must ask yourself why do you hate that person in the first place? And, what part did you play in bringing the events that made you dislike that person into your life?

Who is ultimately responsible?

Brain Washing
07/Jan/2018 07:17 AM

When was the last time that you took the time to cleanse your mind? When was the last time that you took the time to decide to stop thinking the way you always think, do something difference, take control over your mind, and rethink the way you think? When was the last time that you took the time to decide to stop thinking non-stop and silence your mind if even for a moment?

What comes from taking the time to walk a different path than the expected and the accepted is that you come to realize that what is accepted normality is just that, it is the constant. Though it is the constant, by this very definition, it never allows the average person to take the time to find a new and better way of thinking and thereby a new and better way of living life is never discovered. If you never take the time to re-think your life, your life is forever the same. Thus, nothing new is ever experienced on any level.

To this end, the silencing of the mind becomes a conscious and necessary action to discover a new and perhaps better way in which to encounter your life. To do this is fairly simply but you must take the time to consciously stop the commonality of your thought process. You must stop thinking the way you always think. Some call this meditation. That is a fine term if you wish to refer to this process as that. I prefer to call it, silencing the mind.

How do you silence the mind in order to find a new way of thought processing? For each person, this is different. Different things work better for different mindsets.

It must be noted here that some schools of mystical thought make this a very complex and complicated process but it does not have to be like that. I believe that simplicity is always the best antidote. Therefore, to silence your mind all you have to do is to do just that. Sit down or lie down, close your eyes, notice that you are thinking and then simply, with some mental action, wipe those thoughts from your mind. This can be achieved by allowing you mind to turn to black like when a TV or computer screen turns off. It can be a wiping off like with your hand. It can be removing the all or the whatever like when a squeegee goes across the glass of your car's windshield, and so on. It can be whatever you want it to be as long as it consciously causes you to stop your thoughts. Once in this mental space, remain there as long as you can. Let your mind be silent.

This does not have to be a forced thing. There is no time limit that you must achieve. But, the more you do it, the more easily it will be to achieve the *Silent Mind*.

Additionally, there is no expected results that you must achieve; no experience that you must come to find. For each person, it is different. The key is to quest for nothing. From this—from performing this practice—from meeting the Silent Mind, deep realizations about how you think and how you encounter life will be revealed and a whole new of way of thinking may be learned.

Take the time to wash your brain.

* * *

06/Jan/2018 07:33 AM

Of all of the things you believe how much of it is verifiable fact and how much of it is hopeful speculation?

* * *
05/Jan/2018 04:54 PM

Is your life (personally) defined by your mistakes or is your life (personally) defined by your successes?

* * *
05/Jan/2018 04:53 PM

If you have a million dollars and you spend one dollar you are no longer a millionaire.

* * *
05/Jan/2018 04:53 PM

If you don't care what another person does then your life becomes so much easier.

Don't You Feel Bad When You Get It Wrong?
05/Jan/2018 08:10 AM

There are so many people saying so many things and so much of what they say is so not true.

Every now and then I cannot help but take note about all of the false information that people spread across the span of human existence. Though everyone in the Free World certainly has a right to their opinion; an opinion is not a fact as I so often point out. Yet, everyone states what they state, believing what they believe, but if a belief is not based upon a truth than what is the purpose of that belief? It becomes only a tool for a person to use to substantiate their placement in society and to attempt to influence the minds of others.

A belief is a projected ideology used as a replacement for the truth. Thus, it has no absolute meaning. Yet, how many people are intelligent and ideologically coherent enough to realize that fact? Very few. Instead, they take what they have heard, they take what they think, and then they package it and release it as if it were a gift but it is not. It is simply a falsity presented with a bow.

From an academic perspective, people do their research. They find their evidence. Then they present their revelations to a board of other researchers who check and crosscheck this data. Beliefs are never just thrown out there claiming to be substantiated facts. They are only accepted as a fact after a long process of assessment and evaluation.

People, however, find excuses for the falsities they present. They find justifications. They claim free speech. But, if someone is claiming free speech that in and of itself is a sign that what they are presenting has gone through no process of reevaluation by others who possess the qualifications to provide validation and approval. Thus, you must always be weary of what you hear if someone is justifying what they are saying. You must ponder, why are they saying it.

Moreover, do you feel bad when you get something wrong? Do you have any sense of remorse when you have stated something that, through further evaluation, turned out to be wrong? If you don't, what does that say about you?

Life is lived by what we learn. If what we hear, leading to what we learn, is not true, our entire life became a false, baseless existence. If you are contributing to that epidemic, your whole existence becomes the flash point for the demise of not only the other people who have listened to what you have had to say but to the ongoing betterment and evolution of the human race, as well.

A lie is never the truth. A belief that is only believed, is never a fact. Thus, be conscious of what you say and what you put out there, for a false belief you hold, equally a lie you tell, has the potential to not only define your entire existence but the lives of those who have listened to you, as well.

* * *
05/Jan/2018 07:46 AM

You are responsible for the lies that you tell.

*   *   *
05/Jan/2018 07:45 AM

Fame does not necessarily equal money.

Money does not necessarily equal fame.

He's Not One of Us
03/Jan/2018 08:56 AM

"He's not one of us."
"What are you talking about? He's drank blood with the best of us."
"That was in Hell, Marcus! He's never drank blood with us here on Earth."

As a starting point for this blog I thought I would jokingly reference some of the dialogue from my Zen Film, *Samurai Vampire Bikers from Hell,* as it seems appropriate to set up this discourse.

As I am on the Awards Voting board of SAG/Aftra and the Academy I recently watched a screening copy of the movie, *The Big Sick,* which is basically the life story of actor/comedian Kumail Nanijani. I always find it interesting when people play themselves in biopics; i.e. Mohammad Ali, Howard Stern, etc. Anyway, the movie ideally details how people are not only shaped by but live a life defined by their families. I believe that if any of us takes the time to truly view our interrelationship with our family we will see how we were not only molded by them but how we actually mimic much of their behavior; whether intentionally or not. It is only the very strong willed and strong minded who can leave that programming behind if desired. But, few desire to do so.

In life, most people start with their immediate family and then branch out, interact with others, and eventually find their way to forming a family unit of their own. Some people are highly mindful of doing just that. Their entire life is devoted to this process. They meet a person and create a family of their own. In some cases, these are ideal environments. In other cases, they are not. Instead, there is just all kinds of inner turmoil, family fights, and one person or the other being called to the dark side. Yet, blood is blood. And blood usually causes all family members; no matter what crimes they commit, to reunite at the end of the day.

As I've discussed in this blog, I never had much of a family. What this has left me with was/is the ability to step back and watch the goings-on in other families without a lot of predetermined judgments. Good or bad, that has simply been my case.

Rapidly approaching my sixth decade on this planet, there have been a few families I have been closely involved with for a very long period of time. From this, I have watch as certain people have passed through much, if not all, of their life. It has been very enlightening.

As I have also been very closely linked to Korean culture, (a culture which is not my own), for most of life, I have been able to clearly peer into how a new ethnicity to our land assimilates and integrates into a newfound ethos. Sometimes/many times this assimilation is at the cost of the other culture, however. I mean, just for example, how many people do you know who have family members who have come to the country where you live and do not ever learn to speak the native language? I know here in the U.S. that style of behavior is very prevalent. And, that is just one very obvious example.

But, more explanative, I think to an experience I had with the Korean family I have become an extended member of. And, I use the term, *"Member,"* very loosely. I reference this as an interesting example of how the whole family mentality thing has been broadcast and how it affects they ever on-going evolution of life.

A number of years ago my sister-in-law got married. The evening before the wedding my wife and her mother stayed up late into the night making the bridal boutonnieres. My wife, in her first incarnation into the job market, was a floral designer and she was very good. So, the boutonnieres looked very nice. I got to the wedding venue early to help out if necessary and her aunt pins one of the boutonnieres on my suit. Okay, sure... A bit of time goes by, all the boutonnieres had been pinned on the immediate family members, and then arrives one of the cousins. But, no more boutonnieres... My wife's aunt walks up to me and without a word takes the boutonniere off of me and goes and pins it on the cousin. I stood there in disbelief. Then, I got pissed. So pissed, I walked out of the door, got in my Porsche, and was about to drive away. But, thinking to how upset my wife would be if I left, I eventually went back in.

Blood, baby... That's the name of the game... I was not Korean. I was just the white man out...

In any case, sometime before that wedding there had been a major schism in the family. At the root of that family's entire existence, here in the U.S., is one Caucasian man who married a Korean woman, (my wife's aunt), and brought her to the U.S. in 1966; making her one of the very early arrivals of the later massive wave of Koreans that relocated to America. Without him, their family most probably would never have come. One of the newly married members did not want to do anything for the Caucasian patriarch's sixtieth birthday, however, as she was Korean and why should she? Not caring about the legacy he evoked and all... So, until the wedding the two side of the family had split. But, arriving at the wedding came one of the members of the enemy side and BAM, there goes my boutonniere. Again, there I was, another white man, not of the blood. If you look to the family wedding photos, I am the only one not wearing a boutonniere. This, when my wife was the one who actually made them. Interesting... But, no matter what side you were on, they were blood, they were family, they were Korean, and I was not.

  As the years have gone on, I have seen that family grow and multiply and I have witnessed some people die. Years have passed since that wedding. The husband of said female instigator of the family feud stole all his family's money, got deeply into crack, and ran off with a Mexican girl until he had no more money and she got tired of him. Though sidelined for years, he is now back and a functioning part of the family. His son remains arrogant and all-powerful as he lives off his mother's income, under her roof, with no job. It always strikes me as amazing how some people contributing absolutely nothing to anything and yet they still come off as arrogant and feel they have the right to. But, I guess that is just part and parcel to the Korean mind. Anyway, some of the other kids have ended up in college, others in jail, while most of the family members have become successful to varying degrees. But, at the root of all of this is their family bloodline. They never drift too far away from one another. Thus, they choose to take a boutonniere off of one person, who is not of the blood, and pin it on one who is.

I have also witnessed another family I have a long history with, evolve. My one friend's wife passed away and after the appropriate amount of time he had another woman move in with him. The last time I spoke with him he was telling me stories of how they have these intense fights, so much so that he had grabbed the mattress they sleep on and dragged it out to the front yard, throwing in on the dirt. Now, anybody who's in a relationship knows that there will be arguments but damn, that one was big. And, it sounds like that type of melodrama goes on all the time. But, he has his children from the previous wife and that stuff never goes on with them. Again, blood…

I am sure we all have stories like this. Stories about family: what they do, how they do it, and how it affects the future of all those involved. But, at the root of each group is the individual and the choices they make. In fact, everything goes back to the individual and how they participate in the goings-on that are taking place around them.

We are all dealt a hand of cards when it comes to family and to life. Some of us are lucky and find never-ending love. Others of us are left to own device no matter how hard we try to integrate. And perhaps, that is one of the key understandings to embrace as you pass through life. You are you. Yes, you may have a family: large or small or you may have no one. But, at the root of the All and the Everything is that all that exists is you and how you interact with the everything else.

How do you interact? How do you live? How do you think? How do you take? How do you give? How do you exist in the realms of the family: personally or globally?

All there is, is you. What part do you play in the world family? What are you responsible for creating? What are you responsible for destroying? And, what are you responsible for in setting the never-ending course of life evolution into motion?

*   *   *
03/Jan/2018 08:55 AM

Can you see God?

Dead Christmas Trees
02/Jan/2018 07:09 AM

As we come to the end of the holiday season the lights and the decorations are coming down. But, what amazes me more than anything is how people dispose of their Christmas trees. Drive down any street in the city and you will see how people have just thrown them on the curb or tossed them next to a trash bin expecting that someone will pick them up for them. More than simply people's disregard for caring protocol is that fact that, did you ever think about or even ponder the fact that as you picked out that perfect Christmas tree, that it was alive. …That it was a living being and you killed it so you could celebrate a holiday?

Pretty much everyone appreciates a beautiful living tree when you go out into the wilderness. They are exquisite. But, do you think about the fact that either you are cutting down that tree, taking its life, or you are allowing someone else to do it for you, when you buy your yearly Christmas tree?

If you are not thinking about life, you do not care about life. Not just the life of you and your family but the life of everyone and everything.

As a child, we had this silver artificial Christmas tree. I don't know what caused my parents to buy one of those artificial trees back in the early days of their existences but it was a good thing as from this no trees were killed for us to celebrate the holidays. In the 1980s, some forward thinking ecologists became more caring and you could buy Christmas trees alive and in a pot. I did that once. After the season ended I drove up to

Angeles National Forest and planted it. Hopefully it survives and is still doing well.

But, most people do not even think about the life they are taking to celebrate a holiday and then they simply toss their discarded life to the curbside when they are done. This is just not right. I think to all of the devastating fires that have taken place here in California over the past year and all the forestation that has been destroy/that has lost their lives. It is sad. All death is sad. Killing is sad.

Care enough about life to not kill a tree simply so you can put lights and decorations on it and celebrate the holidays.

*   *   *
01/Jan/2018 07:28 AM

What if what you are hearing can only be heard by you?

What if what you are seeing can only be seen by you?

What if what you are saying can only be understood by you?

What Do You Know About Me?
31/Dec/2017 08:44 AM

"What do you know about me?" This is a very perplexing and complicated question in the ongoing understanding of people. Because the truth is, what do you really know at all?

Most people live their lives based upon a mind-statement of judgment. *"I like that person." "That person is pretty." "That person is fashionable." "That person is intelligent." "That person is talented." "That person is good at their job." "That person is ugly." "That person dresses terribly." "That person is cheap." "That person is stupid." "That person has no talent."* But, what does all that mean? Does that mean that you know a person? No, that simply means that you are judging a person and they fall into a definition of a person that you either love or you hate. But, none of that Mind Stuff means that you know that person in any way, shape, or form.

Think about it, how do you operate in your life? Do you see people as they are or do you see people as you project them to be? Do you define people by what you perceive them to be? Or, do you allow them to be whom they are with none of your personal judgment placed upon them?

In life, we each operate from a perspective of Self. We are who we are. We are who we've become. But, if we take the time to study ourselves we can understand why we have ended up in the place where we have arrived in a specific moment of our life. Then, more than simply looking at the building blocks which caused us to become who we are, if we study the way we view, describe, and judge other people we can gain a deeper insight into how we project the reality of our world.

Most people look at other people via the eyes of judgment. Do you?

If you do, you never can know a person at all because you are simply viewing them through your own perception of reality based upon the way you have been indoctrinated into defining others. If you believe and say a person is this or a person is that, what does that say about you? It says you are not seeing them, allowing them to be who they are. Instead, it says you are judging them. Moreover, what makes you think that you are right in your appraisal? Isn't it just your appraisal? But, from this appraisal you set an entire course of events into motion in both the life of the person you have defined but in your own life, as well, because you have chosen to be the one to place your level of judgment onto that other person.

Do you know me? What do you know about me? What do your base your judgments upon? Is it personal interaction in this space and this time? Was it personal interaction from a week, a year, or a decade ago? Am I still that same person or have I changed and evolved? What if you have never met me but you think you know me? How can you know anything about me at all?

Judgment of another person is easy. Whenever a person is talking about and defining another person, this is the perfect time to come to understand who and what that person truly is for from each judgment one can see the flaws and the insecurities of the person who is judging.

In life, we need to live our life. We need to learn, grow, and become the best entity that we can become. This is the pathway to a better Self and

Rising Consciousness. But, judgment should never enters into this pathway. Judgment of other people only distract from the betterment of Personal Self. Thus, anyone who talks about and judges others, defines themselves as a person who is not whole enough in themselves to let other people be whole in themselves.

Exist in your own perfection. Let other people exist in their own perfection. Then, the All, the Everything becomes perfect.

* * *
31/Dec/2017 08:43 AM

If what you are saying isn't nice, what you are saying should not be said.

Hey, YouTube Star, What Are You Doing to Save the World?
29/Dec/2017 02:35 PM

Ever since people found a way to find their celebrity on the internet, it has become a platform for publicity. Though this is not in the exact order of occurrences but first there came websites like Naked News, then personal/explicit website came to be at the forefront of media discussions. The first incarnation of MySpace was a big catalysis for this style of personality driven stardom. Now, sites like YouTube offer a pathway for people to find their fame. But, at the root of this celebrity is one person finding their pathway to recognizable notoriety. Okay... But, the question must be asked. *"Hey, YouTube star, what are you doing to save the world?"*

People forever find a reason to accentuate their life and to make it better. Some people are by nature very outgoing and driven and they seek to be the center of attention. From this, if they have something that the internet masses desire, they may find a pathway to celebrity.

Now, there is nothing wrong in all of this. Throughout modern history some people have desired fame. But, how many people who desire fame ever think about anybody but themselves? How much time do they spend consciously giving back to the world? Sure, most of these people will have an excuse. *"I make people laugh." "People like to look at my naked body." "I tell people what I think and they seem to like it."* Of course, the list goes on. But, how does any of that make this world a better place? How does any of that help the person who is homeless and does not even own a computer or a smartphone? How does that help the people who are devastated by weather or by war? How does that do anything to save the world?

Certainly, there have been celebrities through this modern era who actually stop looking in the mirror, step up to the plate, and go out there and do something that matters—something that truly helps people. How many YouTube celebrities are like that? How many of them get out there, get their hands dirty, and actually help the people in need?

Here are the questions you must ask yourself as you pass through life: *"What am I doing to make the world a better place? What am I doing to help those in need? What am I doing for anyone but myself?"* If you don't have an answer to these questions then the answer is obvious; you are doing nothing. If you are doing nothing, you are doing nothing. You are not trying to help those less fortunate than yourself. If this is the case, why do you feel you deserve any celebrity what so ever?

If you are not doing anything to save the world—if you are not actually trying to help those in need, what does that say about you?

If you want to be famous, be famous for helping people. Then your life will have actually meant something.

The Secrets That You Keep
28/Dec/2017 01:42 PM

Have you ever known a person who got into a long-term relationship with someone but did not tell that person an elemental fact about their past? ...A fact, that if the person knew they may not want to be in a relationship with them at all? Have you ever kept a secret from the person that you were in a relationship with?

This is a complicated issue in that the entire basis of the relationship is based upon a fact that the other person does not know. Yet, if they did know, the relationship may instantly end. In some cases, these relationships may be very happy, very functional entities. Thus, it is felt, there is no reason to create a situation where it may all go array. Yet, in each of these situations, the person who is keeping the secret knows that there are others who know this secret and this must create an enormous amount of interpersonal conflict, worry, and anxiety about the truth being revealed.

I know in my life I have encountered these types of situations. In fact, there have been cases where I did not find out the truth about a person until after they passed away. And, even then, it was by shear accident that I came upon the knowledge. Did this change my attitude towards the person? Absolutely. But mostly, I was shocked that they never told me.

For each person who holds a secret, they have a personal reason for doing so. The causations are many: shame, fear, embarrassment, denial, wanting to project an idealized image of themselves, and the list goes on and on. To them, there is a necessary reason to keep their secret a secret.

On the other side of the coin, there are some people who blurt out anything and everything about their past. Does this cost them relationships? Yes, it does. I have witnessed this. And, I have experienced the necessity to leave a relationship due to choices a person made in their past. I just couldn't accept a person who made those types of choices. But, not everyone is like that. Some people are intrinsically understanding and forgiving.

But here, this brings us back to the central core of the issue. In our life, we each choose to do things. These things may be right and righteous or they may be reckless and fool hearty. But, no matter what the motivation that was present in the moment, we made the choice to do something and every choice we make comes to define the rest of our life. One can say, due to this fact, you must make your choices very carefully as they have the potential to shape your entire future. But, in the moment, many a choice is made that are later regretted.

Ask yourself, does keeping a secret change the reality of what you lived? The answer is, no. But, it may change the way you are perceived by another person. So ultimately, as you pass through your life and choose to reveal or choose to hide what you have experienced, you must understand that the secret does not change the fact of what you lived but a secret may be the only thing that allows you to live the life you want to live.

A truth or a lie, it is a complicated issue.

* * *

28/Dec/2017 12:58 PM

You don't have to like everybody and everybody doesn't have to like you.

Arrogance Before the Fall
28/Dec/2017 07:33 AM

Have you ever encountered a person who is emanating arrogance? They are just totally into themselves. Maybe this is based in a position of power they feel they have developed in life, maybe it is due to the amount of money they have, maybe it is due to beauty, maybe family position, maybe it is because they are full of a self-developed sense of knowing that they are right, or maybe it is simply based in the fact that they are a very insecure person and they use arrogance as a tool to disguise this fact. Whatever the causation factor, they sit there in their own since of developed self-empowerment and broadcast it to the world. *"I hold the power, you do not."*

If we read Proverbs 16:18 it states, *"Prides goes before destruction. A haughty spirit before a fall."* In essence, this can be translated into modern diction as, *"Arrogance or pride comes before the fall."*

Have you ever watched one of those people who bleeds arrogance as they pass through life? Yes, they may hold this position of self-induced eminence for a period of time, but they forever fall. There is no one way this collapse occurs; so, you can't predict or anticipate it. But, it does take place.

Why it takes place also cannot clearly be calculated. Most probably, it is simply due to the fact that this person has no true, inner foundational fortitude for the way they are feeling and behaving and thus, via whatever undefined cosmic method that is out there, they fall prey to their own behavioral patterns.

At the root of this style of behavior is the interpersonal understanding that the person broadcasting it holds, *"I am better than you."* But, who is better than anybody? Yes, some people are born into a better set of life circumstances that may set their tomorrow into a better place. Yes, some people are born pretty, rich, artistic, or athletic which may open doors for them. Some people may simply fall into a career where they excel and rise to the top of their particular game. All of these things and more can give birth to this pattern of arrogant behavior but it is the individual who chooses to behave in this manner. From this is where the distain of other is created and giving birth to.

Do you behave in an arrogant manner? Have you ever behaved in this way? If you have, what was the ultimate outcome to that period of your life and what did it set into motion. Did you come out the others end better, more loved, more respected, or more devastated? If you did embrace arrogance it is certain that the ladder would have been the outcome.

As we pass through life, each of us will encounter those who emanate arrogance. In some cases, these people may cause problems in our life. Instead of being control by their inner-personal self-definition, it is far better to simply ignore or sidestep their mental attacks and leave them to their own eventual demise. For this attitude never leads to a higher self and a better world. It only leads to a moment when a person who is full of themselves is solely defined by themselves but no one else. Thus, the only person who ultimate believes their inflated ego and cares about them is their self. In the end, a person who is defined by this mindset ends up with no one. *"Prides goes before destruction. A haughty spirit before a fall."*

The Things You Know That You Know
27/Dec/2017 09:40 AM

It is interesting, I think, the way people approach life. They know they know what they know but that is all they know. Rarely, do they look any deeper to see what is going on behind the scenes of the obvious.

I look to interpersonal relationships and how people only see the obvious. *"This person is with me." "We are a couple." "We broke up." "It's just casual." "This person cheated on me." "This person left his partner for me." "I'm done! I'm out!"* Of course, this list goes on and on. But, it is all based upon one person's personal perception of the definition of their relationship.

I think to this one person who is in the distant sphere of people I know of... In any case, this woman left her husband stating he was a nice guy but it just wasn't working out. Since then, she has been looking for a new mate. First, she met this really low-end guy. I don't know what she saw in him as he would do things like stand her up on New Year's Eve, have her pay for him and his kids to take a trip to Florida, and so on. Sad... Then, she started going out with this guy she met at work. Deep into the game she finally looked at his Facebook page and realized that he had gotten married while they were supposedly together. When she confronted him about this, the guy, of course, still wanted to do booty-calls, but at least she cut it off. At least, so I hope... I mean, this is a highly educated, pretty, well-positioned person, who should not be treated like this. Yet, she is. But, what fault of it is her own?

Now, this takes us to the crux of the situation. We all perceive reality the way we have been trained to translate it. From this, we base our relationships upon these definitions. The fact is, all those of a particular culture interpret relationships in pretty much the same manner. This is because of the commonality of their upbringing and programming. Sure, there are those who veer off of the beaten path but they are not the norm. Pretty much all people see relationships in the same way.

Within this, there is, of course, those who do what they do with little care for whom they are doing it to; i.e. the guy who got married while never telling his supposed girlfriend. Or the guys (or girls) who cheat on their partner believing there is nothing wrong with that process. Again, this takes us to a person's perception of their own reality. Yet, due to the fact that they are in a relationship, their reality also affects another person's reality.

In modern society there has always been the adoration for the macho guy who parties and pretty much does what he wants. But, the doing, *"What he wants,"* is generally at the expense of the person he is doing it to. Thus, all kinds of hurt, pain, and messed-up karma are given birth to. But again, this goes back to a person's individual perception about how they are calculating reality—how they know what they know.

In terms of relationships, I can think back to my younger years when I was with one person, met another, who I believed may be better suited for me, and was in the process of leaving one relationship for another. At least in my case, one person found out about the other and the transition went completely haywire. Why? Because they projected their own perception of reality onto what was taking place. It wasn't what I was thinking. But, it was what they were thinking. Thus, their reality became the defining reality. And, all things ended. They knew what they knew but did they know anything?

Now, that's just life and that's just the way it goes. But, this all goes back to how we project our understanding onto external situations and onto the minds of others. We see things—we understand things the way we choose to see things and understand things. And, here lies the place to gain new perceptions into the goings-on of relationship. They are a choice.

For anyone who has ever been in a long-term relationship you will understand, it is not always rainbows and kittens. There are disagreements. There is anger. There is frustration. There's fights. But, you make the choice to move through those things. And, that is the essence of staying together; choice. You may know what you think you know but you allow for the other person to know what they know and sometimes you have to allow what they know to set the definition of what comes next.

This is why so many relationships fail. People believe that they know that there is that, *"Something Better,"* out there. As I am sure was the mindset of the aforementioned person I was discussing. But, is there? Again, this mindset is simply the perceived projection of knowing what you believe you know. But, is there actually something better out there or simply more of the same projected in a different and perhaps far less appropriate manner?

So, as you pass through life, you may think you know what you know about the people you know. But, do you actually know? Or, are you simply projecting your own reality and defined perception of that reality onto something that you, in fact, do not understand at all?

You really need to be careful in knowing what you know in life—particularly about other people. As you may not know anything at all.

There Are No Secrets
27/Dec/2017 07:38 AM

Pretty much, across the board, in all art forms: martial art, spiritual, or otherwise, it is always alluded to that there is some super-duper secret that only one person or a very specific group of people know. The chances are you can and will never learn it but if you want to try it will cost you a lot of money to learn from that, *"Master,"* who holds the key. Maybe it is a martial art teacher, maybe it is a guru; but they are they—they know. You are you—you do not. What a great marking ploy! But, is it true? No.

As a martial artist for virtually my entire life, I have seen this type of P.R. going on forever. It has been worded differently, it has been presented in the more obvious to the beyond subtle but the message is the same, there is something super-secret to this training and, *"I am in the only one who can teach it to you."*

On Facebook, I frequently see video presentations about various martial art training sessions and/or professional or street fights that are taking place. Here's the facts. Someone always wins and someone always loses. Do you want to know the secret of the winner? That person hits the other person in such a way that they were the first to disable their opponent. Whether it was a punch, a kick, or a forceful toss to the ground, they did it first and they did it in the most powerfully manner. No secret. That's just the facts of combat.

And, here is where many a martial artist goes wrong on the streets. …This is something I have been writing about for decades. In the studio, you do all this partner training; your opponent attacks this way and you counter that way. Forget it! That is all too pretty. The streets are not like that. They are not even like the sweaty grappling sessions that take place on the mat in jujitsu classes. It is bam, punch, scratch, bite, kick, and roll around on the ground. No training can prepare you for that. Yes, you can prepare your mind, through studio training, in order to keep your wits about you in a fight and plan what you will do next, but there is no secret weapon that you can unleash, taught to you by some advanced master, that will guarantee victory in street combat.

    I saw this so often when Taekwondo swept the shores of the West. There was some practitioner who had beautiful kicking techniques. I mean, they were pretty! They would be all full of themselves in the studio, showing off their kicks. And, maybe in tournaments they also did okay. As in tournaments there are rules. But, the streets are not like that. They would vainly go up against a boxer or a savvy street fighter and one or two punches to the face and they were down. No secret. They just didn't understand the rules of no rules and/or how to fight that kind of a fight.

    Where was the master who held all the secrets and charged them money for years or training? Nowhere. At most, after the fact, all they do is to blame the student and tell them to train harder.

    As far as spirituality goes, here we find an even more complicated game. For in the realms of spirituality, the entire concept is based upon hidden and unobtainable secrets. There is some demigod or guru at the pinnacle. They are the knower. They are the one to be worshiped, as they are the holder of the keys to heaven. But, what do they know that is so unknowable? What passageway have the walked that you have not or cannot? Sure, they may have been doing what they are doing for way longer than you have but what does that actually give them? What it gives them is the time to learn the subtleties of salesmanship. Remember, if they are a teacher, they are a salesman. They are offering you something and getting some sort of reward for it; money or otherwise.

Thus, a spiritual teacher is a liar. They are promising you a something, telling you it is unobtainable, and charging you for that ambiguous knowledge. If lying to you and to themselves is the secret, then yes, they do know it. But, is that true spirituality on any level? No. True spirituality is you give what you know and you charge no fee for it.

The ultimate truth to spirituality and the secret of secrets is, as stated in Zen Buddhism, *"You are already enlightened, you just have to remember that fact."* You can shape that passage to whatever religion you practice and there is the secret to your secret.

In closing, there are no secrets, there are only people who try to tell you that there are so they can charge you money for it to be revealed. The problem is, hand-in-hand with this promise of the secret revelations, comes the caveat, that you will probably never understand it anyway.

Wow, what a great marking ploy. There is a secret but you will probably never be good enough to know it.

Secrets, don't believe them.

The Day After Christmas
26/Dec/2017 10:02 AM

It is the day after Christmas and I am sitting here with a sizeable hangover. I don't know what possessed me but for some foolish reason I decided to drink red wine and beer in tandem all last night at the family Christmas party. One in each hand. I should have realized the impending outcome.

For most people, I think Christmas is a fairly defined period of time of family interaction; some good, some bad. But, you know what to expect... For me, it has never been that way, however. It has always been the abstract expression of, *"Why?"* From this, it has always left me pondering this holiday.

Now, I'm not getting on the religious tip here, as that is not the point of this piece—that's a whole other discussion. This is about the inner-family sort of thing... As was, again, clearly illustrated to me last evening.

First of all, I should begin this dialogue with the fact that I was an only child. In my entire childhood only one family Christmas party ever occurred; attended by my father's family. There, they made me play guitar. I was like six or seven and that is really all I remember about it. You know, being a kid and being forced to do something you don't want to do in front of the masses can be really traumatic. Other than that, my mother, father, and I simply had small Christmases together. As he died when I was ten; that was pretty much the end of that. My mother and I lived in dumpy brick hotels or single apartments. ...That's when she hadn't sent me off to live with some relative, who also had no children. So, my Christmas experiences were fairly bleak.

As I grew through life and entered my twenties, I did spend a few Christmas with my one high school buddy, who married into a pre-made family of two children and then had one of his own. I always found it strange though, as they would give me their Christmas list and my gifts to buy were always the most expensive. But, I didn't really mind. I had a credit card that I was willing to charge-up but it did make me take notice and begin to question the entire point and process of Christmas.

I did that Christmas thing with him until the guy, his wife, and kids left me and my then girlfriend stranded in Bishop, California. He and I had been training his stepson as a bike racer and he insisted I go to this race in Mammoth. Along for the ride was my new girlfriend. We decided to take her car, which broken down. In my friend's own words, *"This is my only vacation."* Thus, I was left fucked. Add to that, though I was the godfather to his daughter, I was not invited to the wedding of his stepdaughter though she called me, *"Uncle Scott."* Which taught me, blood (or at least marriage) is truly thicker than water.

I didn't really do any further Christmas-ing until I got together with my wife. As she is Korean, her family is very religious, and Christmas is a big deal. In the early days, it was okay because her father was a heavy drinking, fun-loving, shit-talking sort of guy, like me. He would get drunk and insult everyone in Korean (including me). We had a lot of laughs.

For those of you who may not know, in Korean-male culture, a man is judged by how much he can drink. Being of Scottish decent, I was right in there. But, he passed away a decade or so ago; lung cancer from smoking and gone was my last drinking buddy. Add that to the fact that the world has now become so politically correct, you just can't say anything without someone reading their own discourse into it and making it something negative. Which brings us to last night...

My wife's sister hates me. I'm told it's because she feels that I stole her sister away from her the better part of thirty years ago and that I remind her too much of her father, who she had a very bad relationship with. I get it, he was an asshole to her. But, there she sat, the first worlds she said to me when I made a joke, *"Inappropriate! That's why you're only invited to these functions once a year." "I'm happy to leave..."* Was my immediate response. In fact, it was a big chore for my wife to even get me to attend. But, my wife would not let me leave. For her, the entire expanse of her childhood was defined by big family Christmas parties each year. Thus, I sat and drank too much.

I spoke with my brother-in-law (my wife's brother) about art and other abstract things, as he is a graffiti artist. I spoke with my other brother in-law (my sister-in-law's husband) about some inside tricks in the film game as he works in the film industry. There was the minor talk about the football game that was on by the other relatives. But, I'm really not into sports... We ate dinner, the kids and family opened their presents. But, as expected, no one gave me anything. No one ever does. And me, I had a wine in one hand, a beer in the other, and I kept that up until I don't remember anything else except falling in the flower garden and killing one of my Armani suits when I got home.

...You say and do a lot of stupid stuff when you're drunk. I mean, somebody has to be the class clown. ☺

So, that's Christmas. At least my Christmas. I'm sure you each had a different experience. Hopefully they were positive experiences.

You know, leading up to Christmas every time you are in the stores you hear Christmas songs. I have heard Chris Rea's, *Driving Home for Christmas* and George Michael's, *Last Christmas* so many times that I want to scream. But, the world, the material world, attempts to drag you into the holiday spirit. But, what is the holiday spirit? And, why is the holiday spirit? For each of us it is defined by how we were educated into it as children. From there, it spreads outwards to those we know, care about, and love. But, I think in each of us, there is some undefined question as to, *"Why?"* Why do we spend the money? Why do we do the get togethers? Why are people invited that we don't like (i.e. me)? Why???

If you don't know why in life you don't know. I think we should all come to a clearer understanding of all of our, *"Why?"* Christmas is one of my big ones...

What Your Actions Cost Others
24/Dec/2017 01:56 PM

I was in the supermarket today, picking up two 12-packs of *Buddha Beer* for a get-together I'm going to. I go and get in the express line, fifteen items or less, thinking that will be the quickest way out the door as the other cashiers had a lot of people buying a lot of stuff. In front of me was this one guy and his daughter. They just had a few things. The problem was, and little did I or anyone else who got in line behind me realize, for whatever reason this guy was going to charge each of these items separately. No, not pay cash but actually charge each of the items on his credit card which meant that each item was going to have to go through the whole process of entering his member ID, having the cashier ring it up, and then inserting his credit card. When he was done with his six or seven items, his daughter started up with her two or three. Unbelievable. The line got massive behind me and I was left standing there in angered disbelief as the cashier, who I know well, kept looking up at me with frustration in her eyes. How can anyone be so inconsiderate?

I imagine that most of you out there would not do something like that. You would be more considerate of others. But, ask yourself, do you ever think about what your actions are going to cost other people? Do you ever question how what you do is going to negatively affect the life of some other person? If you actually ponder this question before you do anything; that makes you a very good, very conscious person. You will certainly go to heaven. But, if you do not ponder this question, if you do not think about others before you do what you do, or if you do things that actually have the potential to hurt someone, you are not a good or a conscious person. In fact, you are just the opposite. You will not be going to heaven.

Living life in a good way is not hard. You simply need to care about others more than you think about yourself. For here is where the fault lies—thinking about yourself instead of caring enough to think about the effect you actions are having on other people. As life is an interactive process, ultimately how you will be judged is how you interacted with those people you encountered.

Who do you want to be in life? The person who cared and helped other people or the person who thinks only about themselves and stands in a supermarket line charging each item separately?

* * *
24/Dec/2017 07:17 AM

If you don't own any books you don't need a bookshelf.

*   *   *

23/Dec/2017 07:41 AM

What you think defines what you live.

What are you thinking?

* * *
22/Dec/2017 02:31 PM

When you buy something used it has been used, you can't expect it to be new.

People are like this too.

Watching the Evolution AKA Everyone's Dead
22/Dec/2017 09:25 AM

There is a new breed of TV stations, offering television series from the early days of TV, that have cropped up recently. Certainly, reruns of old TV shows have been around forever: *Gilligan's Island, I Love Lucy, Gunsmoke, Perry Mason, Bat Man,* and *Star Trek* have never really gone away. But, there were so many other great TV series that, if you weren't there, you would never have known that they existed. These stations are playing some of my childhood favorites like: *Have Gun Will Travel, The Cisco Kid, Rawhide, Wagon Train, The Lone Ranger, Johnny Straccato, Lost in Space, The Rifleman, Naked City, 77 Sunset Strip, Route 66, High Chaparral,* and *Maverick,* onto shows like *Dennis the Menace,* and *Roy Rogers.*

...Did you know that though the *Roy Rogers Show* was supposed to take place in the Old West one of the characters drove around in a jeep? Very strange...

These stations go on to broadcast episodes of shows that shaped my later childhood years, my adolescence, and onwards... Series like: *The Mod Squad, The Green Hornet, The Man from Uncle, It Takes a Thief, The Rat Patrol, Combat, Dragnet, Adam 12, Mannix, The Twilight Zone, The Name of the Game, The Streets of San Francisco, Ironside, Hawaii Five-O, Beretta, The Rockford Files,* and *Hill Street Blues.* Again, if you weren't there, you weren't there and if you don't take the time to watch these shows you may never realize how truly influential they were and how depictive of a time and place in our human history they portray.

But, as I watch them, the one thing that comes to mind is that virtually all of the actors and all of the filmmakers who worked on these shows are now dead. Few, are still alive.

Certainly, this is a condition of life. We all pass on to wherever it is we pass on to. But, if you think about it, these people who are only a generation or two removed from us are now gone. The one factor that allows us to clearly remember who they were is their image having been filmed, which casts their memory to eternity.

Recently, by Zen Filmmaking brother, Conrad Brooks passed away. The day he left us, I begin a piece about him, but I just couldn't bring myself to do. A great man lost. The good news is, if you can call it that, I have told stories about our filmmaking odysseys in other places like in articles and my books on filmmaking and Zen Filmmaking. But, just as in the passing of people like Roger Ellis, Donald G. Jackson, and Robert Z'Dar, the core team of Zen Filmmaking is diminishing rapidly. I'm pretty much all that's left. Most of the others that are still around have left the game altogether. Thinking of these loses does make me sad.

I certainly understand that this is what sets forth evolution. Those who do. Those who take the time to focus and create. Those who for, whatever reason, set about on a path that creates something that is unique and then passed that something onto the masses. Us, we, those of us who do this chronicles a place and a time in history and then set it to something that lasts for more than the moment it was lived within. Thus, it defines a moment of time. Combine this was a life-philosophy, as in Zen Filmmaking or the foundations that created early television, and then there is something that can be looked back upon and, even if you don't appreciate it, you can understand that it defines a something.

For many people, it is hard to watch old television series, as they are not made with the same technological advances and rapid pace of story development that can be seen in today's TV episodes. But, it is like art. For each of us we like what we like, defined by whatever non-rational definitions that rattles around in our brain. But, if we don't take the time to study the evolution, we can never understand why we are where we are and what has brought is to this moment in history.

* * *
21/Dec/2017 04:38 PM

When you do something for somebody do you think you've done enough or do you think about what else you could have done?

Ponder the answer to that question, as it will allow you to see the type of person you truly are.

Maybe you should change?

* * *
21/Dec/2017 04:38 PM

If you were content with what you have right now, what more would you need?

Save the Last Bullet for Yourself
21/Dec/2017 02:13 PM

Homelessness has become a very pervasive issue in America. Not everyone who is homeless is a drug addict or mentally ill, however, though those who suffer from those conditions are most commonly the type of homeless person we each encounter. They are also the most noticeable. There are many others who have simply fallen by the wayside of society. The fact is, it could happen to any of us. I have known very wealthy people who have lost their job and couldn't find another one. In some cases, their spouse left them, taking all their money. Or, they simply overspent, driving themselves deeply into debt and bankruptcy and no one would rent to them. Then, where are they supposed to go?

Coming back from homelessness is nearly impossible. If you don't have a family that will pick you up and help you out, there is pretty much no hope. No hope, unless some miracle happens to you. Other than that, you are pretty much finished.

I was sitting outside, having breakfast, at a local Panera this morning. I always sit outside, rain or shine, if I have the option. This homeless guy walks up and asked me if I could give him any money. I told him that I don't carry cash, which is generally the truth. He immediately then asked me if I would buy him a pair of shoes. It was such a strange request that I just smiled and did not answer. He walked over to the business next to Panera, which is a *Big 5 Sporting Goods*. There he sat down and asked the people walking into the shop if they could help him out as he needed a pair of shoes. He was only wearing a pair of what may be described as shower sandals.

By the time I had finished my breakfast I had made up my mind. I was going to buy him some shoes as no one else was helping him out. I mean, it must be horrible to be homeless with no shoes.

I got up, walked over to him, and asked him what size he wore. *"Eleven."* I went in and bought him a pair of those ankle high hiking boots as I thought those may be the most protective and long-wearing for him. I went out and gave them to him. He was ecstatic, thanking me repeatedly.

I imagine that believing that I would not want to shake his hand, he attempted to give me a fist bump. But, that's all a different generation than me. I reached out my hand and shook his, wishing him all the best and good luck. At least now, he has a pair of shoes.

Think about it, in the world you live in, how many pairs of shoes do you own? And, if you needed another pair, you probably would be able to go and buy them. But, there he was, this relatively young, maybe thirty-year-old guy, who was homeless. He was very coherent and though his clothes were dirty, you could tell he cared enough to keep his hands clean.

What was the cause of his homelessness, I will never know. But, without help, how can he ever regain the things that most of us take for granted.

Like they say in the old movies, *"Save the last bullet for yourself, because if you are captured what will happen to you will be worse than death."* I think that about homelessness. Save the last bullet, because there is virtually no way back.

* * *
20/Dec/2017 03:47 PM

If you are not saying something good then you are saying something bad.

Bad always leads to its own definition.

If you are not doing something good then you are doing something bad.

Bad always leads to its own definition.

When You've Done Something Wrong
20/Dec/2017 12:06 PM

You do not have the right to hurt anyone for any reason.

It is always very interesting to see how people behave when they have done something wrong. This is because, for the most part, no one will ever simply realize that they were at fault, say that they are sorry, try to right their wrong, and fix what they have broken. Instead, they lie, they deny, and they attempt to justify their actions. In fact, in some cases/in many cases, they attempt to blame the other person.

So, what does this say about the person who behaves in this manner? What does this say about their moral code? And, what does this say about the people around them who support them in their justifications, their lying, and their denying about what they have done? What it does provide is a very clear look into the soul of the individual.

Not all people are good and righteous. In fact, very few possess this higher quality.

Businesses behave in this manner all the time. Why are they in business? To make money. So, when someone is not happy with the services they provided, they try every way possible to lie and deny their way out of what they have done so they do not have to refund the money that they charge. But, what they have sold the individual was not what it was claimed to be. It, in fact, may have actually hurt the individual; not to mention diminish their bank account. Yet, does the business owner think about this? No, all they think about is their bottom line.

People are very much like this, as well, though what they do in the hurting of others is not always based upon a financial end-goal. Sometimes people do things that hurt other people by accident. They didn't mean to do it. But, do most own their responsibility in that action—accident or not? No, most people do not. They try to justify and explain their way out of any responsibility. Again, this provides a very clear window into their soul.

Some people actually set out to hurt other people by their words or their deeds. These people are really at the lowest level of humanity. Yet, they are everywhere. Why do they hurt others? There are many reasons for this but desire is probably the biggest culprit. They want something: be it an item, money, human flesh, or being seen as the person in the know. Thus, they speak, they judge, they take. What is the commonality in all of this? Personal desire.

Now, most people do not even realize why they do what they do. They may feel they have the right. They may feel they possess the knowledge. They may feel they possess the power. But, if what they do hurts somebody or something, what they are doing is wrong. It is once this action is done that, again, you truly have the ability to see who and what that person truly is.

As we pass through life, wrong is going to be done to all of us. We are also going to see wrong unleashed onto others. In either/any of these cases, if we watch how the person who has wronged somebody reacts, not only will we be able to understand what kind of person they truly are on the inside but it will allow us to know how they will later react towards others and to us.

People are who they are. It is rare that anyone has the mental fortitude to care enough to make a change.

So, what does all of this tell us? It tells us, don't do wrong things. Don't hurt people, life, or the earth. And, don't support people who hurt other people and do wrong things, no matter what their justification.

If you do hurt someone, if you do something wrong, be whole enough to say you are sorry and try to fix what you have broken. Stop internally justifying your actions because no matter what your justification were, for doing what you did that hurt someone/anyone else, that is only a personal rationalization for you behaving in a manner that did not help the greater good.

How do you feel when somebody does something wrong to you? Let that be the example about how you should behave in life.

Wanting What You Never Received
18/Dec/2017 08:11 AM

As we enter into this holiday season we come to a time of the year where a lot of people are focusing on what they want. Everywhere you go, people are shopping, there is holiday music playing on the sound systems, while ads, flyers, catalogues, and commercials are all advertising holiday deals. Particularly children are making their Christmas lists.

Since we are in this, *"Season,"* even as an adult we are sent to thinking about wants; not only via the lists we have been given by others but what we may want.

Wanting is an interesting emotion. The reason that we want something is that we believe that by receiving it, that item will make our lives better, more happy, more successful, more whatever... It will open a door to that mystical something. Though in some cases we may receive the item we want, in others we do not. When we do not receive the item that we have built our fantasies around, we are forever left wondering what our life would have been like if we had received it.

From a personal perspective, I know as a child, I too had my long list of Christmas desires. Back when I was young, the Sears catalogue was the place where dreams were born. It was a gigantic catalogue. Each year my parents would tell me to circle the toys I wanted. I would go through that catalogue over-and-over again, deciding which ones would be the best. Then, I would circle the desired items. Of course, it was pretty much an exercise in futility, as they never seemed to get me any of the things I wanted. But, from that, I suppose I learned an important lesson in life.

By the time I was a young teenager, and having already found my way to eastern mysticism, I had pretty much given up on wanting things that really did not serve a specific purpose in my life. But, as a musician, there were instruments that I believed would really change my everything. For example, synthesizers were very expensive and pretty much out of reach for a young person. But, the company Korg released what they called the Mini Korg at a very reasonable price; about $300.00. I would go to the music shop that was located on Larchmont Boulevard, all the time to play it. The Christmas season rolled around and I told my mother how important it would be for me to get one; where to buy it, (as there was only that one store in the Hollywood area who had it), how much it cost, and so on. As my mother didn't drive and only took the bus, I even told her how to get to the shop on the bus. Man, I was hopeful… Christmas day arrives, what does she buy me? A Mini Korg synthesizer? No, an autoharp. I was shattered. Though, as I was walking the spiritual path, I did not tell her that. It took me several more years before I could personally afford to buy a synthesizer. I always wondered if I would have gotten that instrument, at that point in my life, what it would have meant to my evolution.

But, that's life. We want what we want but we do not always get it.

Take a moment right now. Close your eyes. Remember that gift you really wanted when you were a child, an adolescent, or an adult and did not receive. For each of us, there is probably one item that will stand out in your mind. Maybe more…

But, for now, focus on that one item. Remember the desire you had for it. Why did you want it? How would it have changed your life if you had received it? As you are older now, imagine how your life would have evolved differently if you would have received it.

Sure, this is all an exercise in fantasy and speculation, but let it play out in your mind. Who would you have been if you had received that gift?

Once you have taken this mental exercise to its completion, open your eyes. Who are you now? What are you now? How well are you living your life based upon the things/the gifts you actually did receive? Did you make the best of every/any gift you received or did you simply receive it and not appreciate it; only wishing you had received that other item you really wanted?

This is the thing about this time of year. For some of us, we will receive gifts. Gifts we may not even want.

What do you do with the gifts you receive? Do you care about the person who gave them to you? Do you care that they took the time to actually go out, earn the money, pay for them, and then give them to you? Or, do you only care about receiving the gifts that you actually wanted and completely dismiss, donate, or throw away the gifts you did not actually want? Moreover, do you only care about the time and money you had to spend on buying the gifts you gave to others?

Getting a gift—the right gift may change your life. Giving a gift—the right gift may change the life of someone else. Think about what you get. Think about what you give to others. As gifts are a life changer.

* * *

17/Dec/2017 08:38 AM

What do you do when you ask god for help and he doesn't answer?

* * *
17/Dec/2017 08:37 AM

What do you do when you realize your fantasies are not going to become a reality?

Coffee House Zen
17/Dec/2017 08:20 AM

Here is another article written for a magazine from the same 1997/1998 period as the previous blog entry.

A friend of mine and myself were at this coffee house in Venice, California last Saturday evening. We were sitting around, taking about life, love, god, and things in general. These two girls came up and sat down next to us. My friend, unattached, became quite exited. This was especially the case when one of the girls leaned over to me and said, *"You look like a Buddhist."* I laughed, because what does a Buddhist look like?

My friend immediately became lost in conversation with the girls. Shortly thereafter, the one who had spoken to me pulls out a cigarette and begins to smoke. She looks over at me, *"I know, I know, a Buddhist shouldn't smoke. I'm bad."* My infatuated friend immediately exclaims, "Don't worry about it. Do whatever you want."

It must be understood, however, *"The do whatever you want,"* mentality works fine in the realms of the material world for in that space of perception you can justify your actions and assign them to the mindset of, *"I'm getting what I want. It makes me feel the way I want to feel."* The realm of a Zen is very different, however, as the mindset of, *"I'm getting what I want. It makes me feel the way I want to feel,"* is completely adverse to that of mindfulness.

The definitions of mindfulness and desire oftentimes becomes blurred in the modern world. The reason for this is because of the fact that within the scope of spirituality there are many conflicting teachings. Some tell you that you can only be holy if you adhere to a very strict vegetarian diet, drink only water and herbal tea, associate with only those of like spiritual mind, and so on. Other teachings detail that you can do whatever you want as long as you do it consciously.

Due to these conflicting teaching, many people become very confused on the path to consciousness. On one hand, they know they are drawn to the spiritual path. On the other hand, they are surrounded and influenced by materialism. As such, they are driven to perform decidedly worldly actions and not only find justifications for them, but realizing that they are doing something not good for their body, their consciousness, the environment, or the world on the whole; criticize themselves. None-the-less, the actions are still performed.

This is the place where many people fall off of the spiritual path. Due to the ease in finding associates who do not share the like mind of spirituality, the world draws one to the dark side.

So, what is the person walking the spiritual path, who is surround by the worldly, supposed to do? If we look at life in regard to mindfulness, the question that must be pondered is quite simple, *"Is what you are doing leading you to a higher state of mind?"* If the answer is, *"Yes,"* then the action may be mindful. If it is not, you are not walking on the path to higher consciousness.

As the actions you take in life are always based upon personal choice—the choices you make sets you on the road to higher consciously, universal understanding, a healthier, happier world, and enlightenment, or they do not. Thus, all things that occur in your life; all the people you meet, and the things that you decide to do in association with those people you meet—all of the outcomes that occur due to the decisions you make are based upon one single choice. What is your one single choice? As that one single choice will come to define your life.

Zen Mindfulness and Can You Remain Mindful When the World is in Chaos Around You?
15/Dec/2017 07:51 AM

I just came upon this article I wrote for a magazine in 1998 and thought it might be helpful.

There is the old adage that it is easy to be holy in a monastery. It is much more difficult to be holy on the streets of the modern world. In addition to this statement being very true, it is also an important factor to keep in mind on your path to mindfulness.

Born in Los Angeles, California, I have been drawn to the spirit of the driven mother ocean as far back as I can remember. Due to this calling, I have lived near her shoreline for virtually my entire adult life.

Having lived in a particular area of Southern California for many years, I would occasionally stroll past this one particular expansive condominium building on my evening walks and think, *"What a perfect place to live. How will I ever be able to afford to live in that building?"*

As if a jokingly given gift was presented to me from the great beyond, a few days after my mother left her physical body, I was looking though the newspaper and found a unit for rent in the building. Though not cheap, it was affordable. Ecstatic, I applied, was accepted, and moved in.

Looking out of my windows I see the expansive Pacific Ocean. Listening, I continually hear the sound of the divine mother's waves.

Though a seemingly idealistic environment, the building is inhabited by a large number of very wealthy people, including an infamous African-

American television evangelist who during the 1960's and 1970's milked an untold number of elderly people out of their life savings—promising heaven if they contributed, hell if they did not. Hand-in-Hand with this affluence comes a definitive problem; the individual units of the building are continually being remolded: floors retiled, carpets torn up and replaced with hardwood floors, design alterations, rooms expanded, and so on... Whereas most of the inhabitants leave for their plush offices or on shopping sprees early in the A.M., before the constructions gets underway, I am left bombarded by a seemingly nonstop barrage of sawing, pounding, and generalized annoyance.

Perhaps the most telling thing about this situation is that during periods of silence, I fall in love with my surroundings. Then, each time I have a project to complete, it seems new construction begins. Thus, I am kept from the peace and solitude and seemingly forced to the necessity of mental focus to the degree where my creativity can be channeled while noise constantly rattles my concentration.

Initially, I became very upset at the noise. I would blame people's desire and vanity, (including my own), karma, god, and anything and anybody else around me. *"How can I be creative with all this noise,"* I would scream.

Somewhere along the pathway I realize, however, that you cannot be reliant upon silence if you wish to remain mindful. Mindfulness cannot be defined by a quiet, passive environment. You must be able to focus your mind to the degree that you can transcend the limitations of the physical world. If you cannot do this, your life, and particularly your mindfulness, will be constantly controlled by your external environment.

Though the noise continues, even as I write these passages, I have been able to create some of my most important work, to date, while living in this building and living through all of the construction turmoil. At some future time, I may move away from this building. For now, I use it as a karmic guru, teaching me to transcend the domination of the material world.

If you choose to walk the path of mindfulness, you must do the same. For if you are only mindful when things are going the way you want them to go, you are not mindful at all. You must be mindful in noise, in chaos, in traffic jams, and in the midst of a heated argument. To do this, you must develop the ability to step back from yourself and remain free of judgment in a world dominated by individualistic desires.

Stepping back, seeing the truth in the chaos, and the perfection in the absurd, this is Zen mindfulness.

Grateful Verse Ungrateful
14/Dec/2017 01:29 PM

Most people are ungrateful for the things that people do for them. This is especially the case if what was done is not on a very physical/material level.

If you buy someone a car, they may thank you. But, if you open a door for them in life, if you teach them some knowledge, if you guide them towards achieving their life goal, if what you do inspires them, it is rare that they will ever acknowledge or even understand the gift.

Think about it… What do you do for the people who have helped you in your life? How do you acknowledge the person or persons who has given you something, taught you something, opened a door for you, gone out of their way to help you, or simply passed on a piece of knowledge that facilitated you becoming a better person? How do you thank them? And, do you thank them at all?

Most people tend to believe that they deserve anything that they receive. Most people are more prone to focus on what they do not have as opposed to what they do receive. Many feel that they are the one doing everything, because they are the one holding the desire. But, this is not true. You cannot become complete unless you are guided towards completion. Maybe it was one of your teachers in school who helped or inspired you. Maybe it was a class you decided to take and the teacher helped you excel in the subject matter. Maybe it was someone who invited you to their table as they knew how to do something that you too wanted to do. Whatever the case, without their help, without their guidance, you would not have been able to achieve what you achieved.

Do you appreciate this fact? Do you acknowledge this fact? Or, do you simple believe you deserved everything that you got? Maybe you even think that they did not give you enough? Or, that you had to work too hard to get it? Or, they said or did something that you did not like, so you rebuke them altogether. But, the question must be asked, without them, without them as a teacher or an inspiration, where would you be?

In some case people don't want to acknowledge the people that have helped them, guided them, and/or given them something. For is they do, that may take all of the spotlight off of themselves. Do you behave like this? If you do, you can never be whole as you are disguising your true influences.

Receiving a gift is easy as the people who give are generally very happy to give. Acknowledging a gift is more complicated. But, if you do not, not only are you lying to the world, you are lying to yourself. Don't be a liar. Respect the people who care enough to give.

* * *
14/Dec/2017 12:04 PM

Honoring a person after they have died serves no purpose, as they are dead and cannot appreciate it.

* * *
14/Dec/2017 12:04 PM

What would happen if you decided to choose a different reality?

* * *

14/Dec/2017 12:03 PM

If you want what you can't have your life will forever be unfulfilled.

* * *
14/Dec/2017 12:02 PM

If you were living in a space where time did not exist, age would not matter.

All the Emotions That Are Lost
14/Dec/2017 06:47 AM

Have you ever had the experience of driving along and somebody cuts you off or does something really stupid in front of your car and you get really mad at them for driving so badly? How long do those emotions last? For the majority of us, it only lasts for a few moments. You are mad, you drive a little farther, listen to the radio, think about something else, and the emotion goes away.

Of course, this situation is also the basis of and for road rage. Here, people get mad and that emotion forces them to do something retaliatory. From this, all kinds of long-lasting negative life situations can be given birth to. But, why do people road rage? Why can they not understand that the anger they are feeling is simply a momentary emotion that will, if they allow it, simply pass away in a short amount of time?

Have you ever had your heart broken by somebody? That emotion can be very intense in the moment of experiencing it. But now, remember that time in your life; whether it was a day, a month, a year, or ten years ago, do you still feel that heart break? No, that emotion is gone. You have moved on.

Have you ever witnessed someone get really mad at another person, causing them to unleash their anger in a very negative manner? What was the result of that? They were mad, they released their anger but what was achieved? All that was achieved was damage and destruction all based upon a momentary emotion. Think how many people have spent their life in jail due to falling prey to this style of emotional reaction.

Have you ever really liked someone that has come into your life? But, then time moved along and you began to see deeper into their psyche and you realized you really didn't like who that person is so you broke ties with them? Were they any different or did they simple emerge as the person they always were? Your emotions of like, attraction, or respect brought you to them but then your emotion of realization, based upon personal interaction, cause you to move away.

Think about a time when you were really happy in your life. Think about where you were, what you were doing and/or whom you were doing it with. In that moment of happiness, all was right with the world. But, what happened to that emotion? It was lived, it was felt, but now it is gone.

You are your emotions. How you experience your emotions, how you interact with your emotions, how you control or do not control your emotions comes to be one of the elemental defining factors of your life. But, the key component you must understand is, your emotions are your emotions. They are not the emotions of anyone else. What you feel is not what someone else is feeling. For example, the person who cut you off when you were driving; are they feeling anger at what they just did? No. They probably do not even realize what occurred. Is the person who broke up with you experiencing your emotions? No. They are lost in their own set of emotions that is causing them to leave you.

Emotions are felt and then they are gone. What does that tell you about the experience of emotions? It shows you how impermanent they are. Should you guide your life dominated by something so impermanent as emotions?

Whatever your emotions may be, at any given moment of your life, it is only you who feels them. You feel them, you do what you do based upon them, but then time and your life moves along and they are gone. Thus, you should be careful to never lose yourself in your emotions for something so temporary is a very deceptive master.

* * *

13/Dec/2017 06:46 AM

If you are honest and you know what you know you say, *"I know."*

If you are honest and you don't know you say, *"I don't know."*

If you are dishonest and you don't know you say, *"I know,"* when all you are stating is based upon your belief.

Belief is nothing more than you wanting something to be something but it is not.

* * *
13/Dec/2017 06:44 AM

You can sit back and do nothing.

You can stand up and do everything.

But, if what you do has no absolute meaning, what is the difference?

*   *   *
13/Dec/2017 06:41 AM

Your actions have consequences.

What consequences will you be facing for the actions you will be taking today?

**Babble and the Mindless Trouble
That People Create**
12/Dec/2017 09:07 AM

As a pastime, I sometimes write reviews for various travel websites telling the tales about my experiences at places I have traveled to, ate at, or stay at in order to help those people who may travel there after me. From this, sometimes I am asked by the administrators of these sites if I can answer a specific question that someone has asked about some place or location. Most of them are very straight forward questions. But, in some cases, they are simply ridiculous.

Recently, I received a question about this place I had traveled to in Iceland. But, the guy asking was completely off his rocker. It wasn't so much a question as it was a statement completely making things up about how he had gotten very sick at this place, etc. But, the fact is, what he claimed he ingested was not possible at this place. Me, I just blew off the question as why waste my time? But, I did notice that there were a number of people who got into the whole debate as what could or could not have taken place.

Why waste your life time?

This is the thing that I have long realized about life. There are those people who live life, do what they do, help those they can, when they can, and cause no intentional problems or conflict. Then, there are those who have no self-awareness—maybe they hate themselves or their life, so they go out into a world like the internet, where there will be no repercussion for their antagonistic actions, and cause trouble. But, to what end? How does any of that make anything any better?

You know, if you help somebody, you help them. All is good with the world. If you hurt somebody, you hurt them. You will be remembered by that person, in a very negative way, forever. But, if you mess with people's life and people's life time from afar, for no good reason, all you do is create a lot of negative energy emulating around yourself. This is why so many people's lives remain lost.

What you choose to expound from you, you evoke in your life. If it is good, it is good. If it is bad, it is bad. If it is ridiculous nonsense that serves no better person than to drag people into a nonsensical discussion than by wasting everyone's time you have created a wave of negativity that will be redirected at you.

Life is your choice. It is your choice what you say and what you do. What do you do? And, do you allow yourself to be dragged into any person's wave of unconstructive babble just because you hear or see something that they have said? Or, do you focus only on a positive road that helps all those you encounter?

*   *   *
12/Dec/2017 08:38 AM

Is an accusation the truth?

Is It Good for the Greater Good?
12/Dec/2017 07:41 AM

Last night, at about 4:00 AM or so, I looked out over the horizon. To my right I could see the orange glow of the fire that is raging in Venture and Santa Barbara County lighting the sky up above the Santa Monica Mountains. I then looked around and off in the distance I could see a cruise liner, obviously full of passengers, apparently having a good time as they are taking a cruise. What a dichotomy. In one place, there are firefighters risking their lives to keep homes from burning and in another, just a few short miles away, there are people paying a lot of money to take a vacation and thinking about nobody but themselves. This is a very good example of life.

For those of you who may not know, currently, there are a number of fires burning around Southern California. Just like the Santa Maria, California fire of a couple of months ago, they are very devastating. Caused by global warming, the large amount of rain we received last year ending the drought and causing a lot of new vegetation to grow, or simple the stupid action of some individual—whatever the cause, life and property has been lost.

I have always had the utmost respect for firemen. They put their lives on the line every time they go to work. They care. They take action. They do what needs to be done in the most conscious way possible to save lives and property. They are true heroes. Most people aren't like that, however. They only do for themselves. They only do to do thing to get the things that they want. Even if they are doing something that they believe is good for the greater whole, their own ideology is at the heart of what they are doing. So, is what they are doing actually for the greater good or is it simply what they believe is the greater good?

I watched a documentary about Julian Assange last night. He is an ideal example of this mindset. Now, whatever you think about him and his actions is whatever you think about him and his actions. I have my opinion. But, that's not the point. He did what he did which landed him hiding out in the Ecuadorian embassy in London for the past several years. He's a prisoner. But, the question must be asked? Have the things that he has done, which have cost him his freedom, truly changed anything? Yes, he may have revealed some things unknown to the masses but has the world changed because of his actions? I don't believe it has. There is still fires and there are still people taking cruises. There are still governments doing all the clandestine things that governments do. This, while he is trapped.

Now, there have been people who have operated on a similar platform. Whether is was Nelson Mandela fighting for the rights of the native Africans in South Africa. ...He spent decades in jail for his actions. Aung San Suu Kyi who spent years under house arrest in Myanmar. ...And now, look at the devastation that this Buddhist regime brought to the life to the Rohingya, Muslim minority. Gandhi who was assassinated for who he was and what he believed. Did these people instigate change? Yes, maybe… At least, like Assange, they are well portrayed in movies. But, was it actually them who instigated change? And, was the price they paid worth being the visual figurehead for a movement?

I mean, the truth be told, in terms of South Africa, Steven Van Zandt had a large hand in aiding in its change as he got together a bunch of rock stars of the era and they did a popular song that really shifted the world's thinking about the country which helped in causing apartheid to fall. And, he did that without going to jail.

Think about all the people who have tried to help those in Africa over the years. They did this while cameras rolled on them. But, what has truly changed? Virtually the entire continent is a geopolitical, humanitarian mess.

The point being is that people care when they have a reason to care. Very few ever care simply to care and they do not care if it does not affect their life in a positive manner. For example, in the Assange documentary, you can see that he is worshiped by some of his people. Thus, though their actions are perhaps based upon a commonality of cause, there is the interplay of human emotion locked into each of these actions. So, the question must be asked, who is doing what for whom and why?

If you look at yourself, who cares about you? Most probably, the people who know and love you.

Do you care about me? And, I use, *"Me,"* as a generic me. You don't know me, but do you care about me? Do you do anything for me? Do you care what happens to me? Some would say if you don't, that means that you don't care. What does that say about you?

This life is filled with million upon millions of people. If you live in a city, think how many people you see every day that you do not know. Do you care about them? Do you give them a second thought? And, are any of the things that you do geared towards making any body's any thing any better? Or, do you simply take a cruise on a cruise ship while the fire's rage?

Who You Can Never Be
11/Dec/2017 09:23 AM

People desire to BE something. They desire to BECOME what they want to become. Whereas most keep these desires well within a life perspective, others step beyond the bounds of their defined reality to achieve their desired end-goal. From this, yes, certain people do rise above the rest and achieve what they see themselves as becoming but many of these people achieve what they achieve without ever deserving the achievement they accomplish.

Let's look at this condition a little bit deeper…

Since the rising of the New Age, in the 1960s, people became very outspoken as to not only what they were feeling but broadcasting what they, personally, believed. From this, certainly a change in culture was given birth to but also a false narrative was also born in that people believed that by somehow stating who they think they are and then telling people the faults they see within themselves and others that it somehow endears them to people, society, and the greater world as a whole. But, there is a flaw in this ideology. That flaw is, people only care about anybody if they have a reason to care about them. Now, this reason may be desire: physical, emotional, sexual, or psychological. But, whatever the invoking clause, if someone does not care, they do not care and, thereby, by telling anybody, anything about yourself you complete destroy the purpose of self-evaluation and are simply lost into a space of ego believing that someone out-there should care about the person you are in-there.

Certainly, with the dawning of the age of the internet, people have been able to make vast steps towards becoming what they see themselves as via self-motivated and self-developed publicity. No longer does a person have to first be accepted by a person or a group who would then train them and lead them, in a focused manner, up the ladder of achieving their interpersonal desire. They could just do it on their own. But, in this process of self-motivated emancipation, something has been lost. No longer is there checks and balances about what is good, bad, mediocre, and/or even dangerous. People just personally spread the ideology that they are *Someone who is Something* saying what should be heard. And, they do this without ever gaining approval of the established hierarchy.

From the anarchist's point of view and from the point of view of the person who desires fame, fortune, and massive acknowledgement, they believe they have found the keys to the kingdom. But, the problem is, in many cases this person may look the part, speak the part, but they are not qualified to inhabit the level of notoriety they achieve. Maybe they don't have the education, maybe they don't hold the credentials, maybe they are just a vain person who feels that they are something and they deserve adoration for what they believe they know. Any of these can give birth to this but at the core of any person's desire of achievement is their own ego telling them that they have something that someone else needs. By this very definition, however, they do not possess the actual qualifications to hold that position as what they believe is only based upon their interpersonal definition of Self. Thus, no matter what they achieve, it is not based upon truth but simply a misdirected ego.

If we look to history, we can easily see, even in recent times, how people who should never have been in control of the minds of others, have risen to prominence simply by them believing that they, themselves, have something that should be heard or should be seen. Charlie Manson was an ideal example of this. Pol Pot was another. …As are all of the religious zealots, from all of the religions across the globe, who are attacking those of other faiths and other sects. Just watch the news and you will see the heart-breaking devastation the people who are supposedly basing their lives upon the words of god are unleashing. They are people who believe that what <u>they</u> believe should be heard and should be practiced.

Certainly, most people who desire to find the eyes and the ears of the masses are not that diabolical. But, if any of these people look at themselves they will not be able to deny that the reason that this wish to be in the public eye is that they believe they have something to say worth saying and/or something to see worth seeing. Thus, all they do is based upon their belief in themselves. Thus, their entire life is based upon their own ego.

Do you want to give credence to and follow someone like that?

* * *

11/Dec/2017 07:46 AM

If you are hungry, have no money, and someone buys you a meal, they are a saint.

* * *
11/Dec/2017 07:45 AM

You should always take a look at your own life and define what is right and what is wrong with yourself before you ever judge anyone else.

Wanting Something More
11/Dec/2017 07:34 AM

As we enter into this Christmas season, we come to a point where a lot of people are thinking about what they want and expressing it to others. It is also a time when people come upon things that they may desire, not even knowing that they wanted it until they see it, and then set about on a course of getting it. Mostly, it is a time where it seems okay to express your desires—to tell people what you want and to go after getting whatever it is you may have a yearning for.

Is there anything bad about this? Well, not really... Certainly, we all should understand that we should know better than to spend more than we can afford. I mean, don't charge anything on your credit card that you can't pay off at the end of the month and stuff like that... But, none-the-less, this seemingly is the time when you can crystalize your desires.

For each of us, throughout our life, we desire what we desire. As the great author and visionary Ken Kesey defined it, *"Current fantasy."* Meaning, we want what we want when we want it. But then, we either get it and desire it no more or that fantasy fades away. Yet, in the moment of wanting (Something-Anything) we are trapped and held by that desire.

Yet, think about it, getting that thing that you want feels great! Whether it is a hug from someone you love, the first touch of a new lover, or receiving that thing you dreamed about and/or really needed, it is a glorious feeling to get what you want. But, that getting may come to be the definition of some people's lives and from that they are cast into a space of never-ending wanting more.

Keep in mind, however, there may arise a problem in this process of wanting. That problem is, what if you don't get what you want? Ask yourself, *"If you don't get what you want how do you deal with it?"* For how you deal with this emotion, sets the stage for your entire life.

As each of us passes through life, we are allowed to come to a clearer understanding of the, *"Wanting what we want,"* syndrome. For most of us, there are times when we want something and do not get it. This provides us with a great learning experience as we can come to terms with the realities of life. The reality that none of us are going to get everything that we want. But, just like a child, some adults never take the time to step into a world of realization and they get angry, yell, scream, and throw tantrums when they do not get what they want. Do you?

On the other side of the coin, for those with a mindset geared towards self realization, it is also a time to come to terms with the reality that getting what you want is not the end-all to your life.

How many times have you gotten something you desired and it really messed you up? Maybe it was being in a relationship with a person that turned bad, maybe it was that motorcycle that you got into accident on and really damaged your body, maybe it was getting a book that you read, believed, and it guided you down the wrong road in life. The list is endless. But again, for those with a mind for self contemplation, you can easily realize that getting what you want is never the absolute solution to living the life that you desire.

So, I guess the point of all of this is, you really need to be whole and adult enough to chart your desires in life and allow them to be defined by what is truly and actually available to you at whatever stage of life you find yourself in. Never allow yourself to be controlled by your desires. Because <u>your</u> desires are only <u>your</u> desires. They may be what you want but may very well be what no one else wants.

* * *

06/Dec/2017 09:25 AM

Why does anyone want anything bad to happen to anybody?

Want to See Yourself on TV
AKA Fame and the Cost Thereof
06/Dec/2017 08:20 AM

Being a film producer, (admittedly on the very low-budget side of the equation), I have met so many actors and actresses that all hold the same dream, to be seen on the silver screen; i.e. to be famous, respected, and adorned by the masses. They all speak the same words, that it is <u>they</u> who is going to, *"Make it."*

By my nature, I believe in people. But, by my nature, (due to my long-list of life experiences), I am also very skeptical about the motivations for people doing what they do and what they will do to get what they want. I have seen a lot. I have experienced a lot of people doing very bad things to gain the level of life that they desire—they don't care who they hurt in the process.

People, by their nature, are a vain breed. They do what they do, to gain what it is that they want. They do this at all levels of life. And, here lies the problem with humanity.

This being said, of all these people who make all of these proclamations—of the ones I have encountered, virtually none of them have ever risen to the level they desired. Yet, in their wake they have left a lot of damage. The one's that did gain a foothold, did so by not burning their bridges and not disrespecting the people who helped them on their path. Thus, it is really those who accept help, appreciate the help, and then repay the help with each step they take that have moved up the ladder.

As the dawning of the digital/internet age came upon us, it was much easier for people to grab the foothold they hoped for—getting their face known by the masses. They could buy a video camera, get a computer, and do it themselves. But, this takes intense focus and personal motivation. Few people possess that quality. But, more than that, it takes the ability to be calculating enough to plug what you do into a specific mindset where it will be appreciate. Just as so many people come to Hollywood to find fame, so too the person on the internet must find an audience that wants to watch them or their game plan will fail.

As Reality TV took hold across the globe, many people began to emulate this style of antics in the home productions they produced. One of the key factors for gaining any success was doing something that people wanted to watch. Certainly, the early interpersonal, *"See me naked,"* stuff was a big hit on the internet. But, as time when on there were some people who were very calculating in the portrayal of themselves which gained them an audience without being so blatant in their production. One of the things that used to amuse me no end, and I guess still does, is when young women would do their video presentations from their bedroom. BAM! They instantly had audience. Why? Because every young guy out there, dreaming of having a girlfriend, now has a point of focus. They can see the girl, see where she sleeps, and this sets all kinds of fantasies into motion.

I have long warned women, who do this type of production to be very careful, as they are opening up their inner sanctum to the eyes of the masses. They are giving everyone a map of their existence. Though most who would watch these productions are just young boys lost in a fantasy, some people are far more diabolical than this. Thus, problems can be born.

This is no different from the actresses I have known who pass their address out to anyone in the industry that they meet and they live in a ground floor apartment in the junky part of town. Don't do it! Get a P.O. Box!

As the whole, *"Casting Couch Empire,"* here in Hollywood has begun to crash down, via the #metoo campaign and other factors, it was revealed to the masses all the goings on. But, this style of behavior goes on everywhere. Will it change? We can hope… But, probably not. Again, people are a vain breed willing to do whatever it takes to get what they want.

So, the point being… People desire fame. People blindly pursue fame. If this is your case… First of all, you truly should look insides of yourself and decide why you want that fame? What is motivating you to gain that fame? What will it mean to you, to your life, and to the rest of the world, if you do achieve that fame? Because there is always a price to pay.

Moreover, if you do gain any notoriety, what are you going to do with it? Because the fact is, if you do gain some notoriety you can help people with it or you can hurt people with it. For example, people with notoriety (large and small) have done both to me: helped me and hurt me. I mean, people I've never met have done things to me that have damaged my life, but to what end? Did it make the world any better? And, I'm just using me as an example as this stuff goes on all around us, to everyone. If hurting or judging someone only made them feel better than something has been lost from this entire equation as then the source point for their desire for fame has been revealed; personal power.

But, from personal power always come war. And, war has the potential to destroy everything.

There is a good documentary about the actor/comedian/activist Russell Brand. Watch it if you get a chance because it really documents how a person with an insane level of ego attempts to walk the spiritual path and make the world a better place. You can judge it and him as you will. But, that documentary is an ideal example of a person who came from little but rose to the top of public view and you can see what it did to him and what he did with that power.

This is the thing, and back to the point, with any notoriety comes responsibility. If you have notoriety and you say or do bad things—if you hurt anyone there will always be a karmic price to pay somewhere down the line. The bigger hurt you inflict, the bigger the payback. Just as if you help. The bigger the help, the better the world becomes—including your world.

So, in conclusion, why do you want what you want? And, what are going to do with what you get?

Buddha on the Net
05/Dec/2017 07:48 AM

In some/many ways it surprises me how many people have been reading what I have been writing on the world wide web since its inception—way back in the way back when. Recently, I've been receiving several questions about what happened to and why did it happen to a site I used to have titled, Buddha on the Net.

Basically, Buddha on the Net was a page devoted to spiritual links around the internet.

To answer the question(s), the main reason I took it down was that it became so hard to maintain control over how the various sites I linked to changed, some overnight, into sites that were not at all spiritual.

Just a side note here... I also used to have a page (way back in the way back when) that provided links to the various martial arts sites around the internet. But, that was before there were millions-and-millions of them. And again, I eventually took it down for the same reason stated above.

In any case, I remember receiving a deluge of this same question being asked several years ago. I wrote a piece about it in the first Scott Shaw Zen Blog that was eventually published in the book, Scribbles on the Restroom Wall. Anyway, that's the answer and just for the memories here's the original piece...

Buddha on the Net

Before the Internet was even called the Internet, and before scottshaw.com, I had two pages up in the early stages of what later became known as the World Wide Web. One was, The History of the Korean Martial Arts and the second was a page providing links to spiritual pages, eventually titled, Buddha on the Net.

The History of the Korean Martial Arts I put up because I was one of the first to truly study and document the modern evolution of the Korean martial arts. And, as I have long said, *"The original masters have continued to change their stories."* So, I hoped to place a frame of reference of the history and evolution of these modern schools of self-defense.

Buddha on the Net I created to provide people who were interested in studying or following the spiritual path a means to investigate the various sources of information and the schools.

Approximately one year ago, I did a complete redesign of my website. What I had come to realize, regarding Buddha on the Net and links to other sites, is that I had no control over their content. Some sites would change and some began to propagate very negative ideologies. Some began to spew malware. Following in my own philosophy, *"You can only play in your own playground,"* I decided it was best to take down Buddha on the Net, as well as other pages on my site that provided links to other sites, as I had no control over what they had to say.

Recently, due to all the requests and questions of, *"What happened to Buddha on the Net,"* I have decided to put it back up on scottshaw.com.

So, Buddha on the Net is back up, providing links to spiritual sites. I trust you will find it helpful.

Post Script: That was then but I quickly came to realize that I ran into the same problems so Buddha on the Net was just re-up for a short amount of time and then, like Zen, it became an undefined illusion.

That's the story… Be positive and smile. #bepositive ☺

Why Do You Say What You Say?
05/Dec/2017 06:38 AM

Why do you say what you say? Why do you behave in the manner that you behave? Most people never take the time to question this in themselves. From this, they do not live in a space of truth. They simply live a life based upon undefined emotional reactions.

Right now, take a look at yourself. Why do you say the things that you say in the manner that you speak them?

If you take a moment and truly study this quality of yourself, you will quickly come to understand that you say the same words, using the same verbal patterns, over and over again. Why do you do this?

Right now, take a look at yourself. Why do you behave in the manner that you behave?

If you take a moment and truly study the way you behave, you will quickly come to understand that you behave in the same way to all of the people that you meet. You begin your interaction based upon a certain set of behavioral patterns and you continued forward through the relationship behaving in a specific pattern. You do this until the relationship ends in the same way your other relationships have ended. But, why do you do this?

Now, many people will pass this off as simply, *"That's just who I am,"* or, *"That's just my personality."* But, if this is your answer, that again brings us back to the fact that you are not living an existence based upon truth, you are simply living a life based upon emotional reactions created by and from whatever source. But, by dismissing the fact that you can and do have a responsibly in what you say and what you do, you are not living an existence defined by interpersonal understanding and control. Instead, you are simply living a reactionary life based upon your undefined human emotions.

Okay, so what are you going to do about this? That is a personal choice. First of all, most people never even question the way they are behaving—why they are thinking what they are thinking and why they are saying what they are saying. But, this is life operating from a very unenlightened point of view. Again, what are you going to do about this? The answer is, if you choose to truly be whole, complete, and raise your consciousness to a higher level of understanding and human/interpersonal interaction you have to begin to chart out and define why you say what you say, the way you say it, and why you behave the way you behave. These conclusions are not hard to reach. But, if you don't look, you won't find. Then, once you have found the answer, it is only you who can choose to take control over your life and guide it in an enlightened direction where misguided or judgmental emotions are not your common motivation for the way you speak and act.

You can be more than the words your unrefined mind makes you speak. You can be more than the way your undefined behavior makes you behave.

Looking for Your Fifteen Minutes
04/Dec/2017 04:47 PM

What god do you worship?

Now, this may seem like a strange question in this day and age but if you look around yourself, if you look inside of yourself, if you truly analyze the lives and the motivations of those who speak the loudest—those you turn to for advice, you may be able to see that those you look to for guidance are the ones you should never look to for guidance.

Who writes the doctrines? Who writes the reviews? Is it somebody who has lived the path or is it someone who sits back and simply has the enhanced ability to discuss what they like and/or do not like—what they think about what they think about?

You know… If you have ever painted a painting, you know what it is like to paint a painting. Is it easy? No. You have to buy the paint, you have to buy the canvas, and more than all of that, you have to possess the inspiration and the drive to take what is in your mind and place it upon that canvas. How many people possess that ability? Very few. But, how many people are out there who can tell you what they do or do not like about a specific painting? There are many. But, are they an artist—are they a true creator? No, they are not.

At the root/at the heart of art is the artist. At the root/at the heart of everything else is criticism—instigated by those who cannot create art. Yet, they are the ones who verbalize what they think and feel. And moreover, there are those who are out there who possess no personal understanding of what they should or should not think and feel. Thus, they are the ones who listen to the words of these supposed pundits and they base their entire life upon what these people say. From this mindset, they do not base their existence upon true, personal realization. Instead, they based their life upon the contrived knowledge dished out by someone who does not possess an enlightened, self-realized understanding about what they speak.

If someone calls themselves a pundit, they are anything but a pundit.

If someone lives their existence by critique and criticism, that is all they are. If that is all they are, why should you listen to them for all they are doing is basing their existence upon the creations of others?

Why do they do this? So they can gain their fifteen minutes of fame based upon the artistic inspiration of someone else.

Why do people critique and criticize? Why? Because they have no inner inspiration. They are not the artist. All they are is the person who wants to make a name for themselves based upon the inspiration of the true artist.

*   *   *
04/Dec/2017 04:36 PM

Say good things. Do good things.

* * *
04/Dec/2017 09:25 AM

Just because you wear a cross around your neck that does not mean that you are a true Christian.

* * *
04/Dec/2017 06:49 AM

Do cats have a name for the color green?

* * *

03/Dec/2017 04:31 PM

When you die, how will your life be remembered?

...Is your answer a realistic appraisal or is it only a pipe dream?

* * *
03/Dec/2017 03:33 PM

If all you do is think about and discuss what other people have done then all your life will be defined by is what other people have accomplished.

* * *

02/Dec/2017 03:41 PM

All of the experiences in your life makes you who you are but is who you are who you want to be?

The Art of Denial
01/Dec/2017 08:47 AM

Have you ever had somebody do something to you that was really messed up but then they totally denied doing it? I imagine most of us have had that experience in one way or another.

Some of these things are small and just a minor irritant. Others, are big and really mess with our life. But then, the person who is responsible for the action totally lies, justifies, and denies their responsibility in its doing. Thus, they practice, *"The Art of Denial."*

You know, everybody has a reason for doing what they are doing. At least in their own mind, what they are doing is being done for the, *"Right,"* reason. But, is it? Is what they are thinking a conscious thought or simply a thought based in a preconceived notion about how they personally calculate their own reality?

On one hand, there are people who really try to make a positive difference in the world and truly attempt to actually help people. What they do is generally done from a perspective of good-ness. But then, there are those people on a mission. They do what they do believing that what they say and the way they think and act is right. Maybe they feel that what someone else is doing is wrong. Maybe they feel they have the right to, *"Call out,"* somebody. Maybe they just think that their opinion matters more than anyone else's, so they do some-thing to some-person. But, by believing that what they, themselves, are thinking and what they are feeling is right, (more right than what any other person is thinking and believing), that means that they are not operating from a clear and whole mindset based in a universal understanding of true reality. And thus, when people act based upon this mentality, they hurt the life of other people. Whether they believe they have the right to do it or not is irrelevant. Hurting on any level only causes hurt. Thus, nothing whole and/or good is ever born from that action.

This type and style of belief permeates our existence. Think of all of the religious zealots out there who base all that they do upon judgment. Think about the Average Joe who critiques and criticizes all that they do not understand.

Certainly, this denial mind-style goes to the concrete realms of reality, as well. Think about the mechanic who fixes something in your car but it doesn't correct the problem. You still must pay for their mistake of mechanical understanding. Yet, they most assuredly will lie, deny, and justify what they did and why they did. But, the problem is not fixed. At best, you will have to pay more to get the actual problem corrected. This recently occurred to me to the tune of over a thousand dollars.

People also go into the mindset of denial about concrete reality to buffer themselves from taking responsibility from their accidents or misdeeds. A little while back, a guy ran into the back of my lady's car because he was messing with his phone. He ran into the back of her car, shoving it into the car in front of her. Though he admitted his fault to us, he lied to his insurance saying it wasn't his fault. I mean come on… So now, the insurances companies get to play the game of doing what they do and taking the matter to arbitration. Like I always tell people, keep your deductible very low that way you will not encounter the need to lie. But, lie and deny he did. What is the karma for that?

And, this is what it all boils down to: truth verses lies.

Why do people do bad things to other people? They do them because they are only thinking about themselves. They do them because they do not care about anyone else or they would not be trying to hurt them and then they would not be denying their responsibility in what they have said or done.

If you encounter people in life, on any level, there will be interpersonal interaction. But, it is you who decides to be truthfully in the moment with all those you encounter or not. We all make mistakes in life. We all do things that perhaps another person does not like. But, first of all, we must chart our life to consciously avoid that style of behavior as best as possible. Then, if we do interact with someone and the situation does not turnout mutually amicable, we must be whole and understanding enough to take the other person's point of perception into consideration and never deny our responsibility it what has been done.

Any doing, makes the doing, your responsibility. Own the reaction.

*   *   *
30/Nov/2017 08:46 AM

When you tear a piece of paper it can't be untorn.

Late in the Late Night
30/Nov/2017 03:49 AM

I was staying up way too late in the late night as I tend to do. It is rare that I go to bed before... Well, before way too late in the late night... It has always been this way with me. Though I love sleep, I sleep very little.

Anyway, I was pounding down another bottle of wine and trying to find something worth watching on the thousands of TV station and On Demand programs I have at my access when I came upon a TV show on a PBS station where they were playing music video from the 1980s. It came complete with the one-time MTV VJ Martha Quinn. I watched a few and then thought about this other MTV station that plays flashback videos. There I sat, flipping between the two stations; both lost in the 1980s. A time when the music video was king.

Now, for those of you who were not alive at that period of time, it may be hard for you to imagine or understand but music videos were really changing the way we viewed the world. In fact, it was so important that you saw what was new—what was being portrayed in those visual images...

I remember a time when I was living in Hermosa Beach—a time when video recorders and MTV were new—a time when I would sit there in the afternoon, drinking coffee, drinking wine, painting these very large paintings, and hurrying to record any new video that came upon the screen. It seemed so important back then...

But, as I sat there watching them tonight, it was such a reminder of a time... A time when there was actually a, *"Fashion,"* a, *"Style,"* in the world. There was an essence that was being portrayed in existence. And, that fashion was an essential element of the music.

Now, I am not sitting here being nostalgic, as that is really not who I am. What I am sitting here stating is that there are points in history when fashion defines culture and from that art is born. Certainly, we are not in a period like that here in 2017. It is just a mishmash of the nothing. …Of the accept and the acceptable. But, it was not always like that.

I feel very honored to have been a young boy in the 1960s when culture changed. …A young man in the 1970s when you could be anything that you wanted to be. And, a young adult in the 1980s when style swept the planet. I remember my days in West Hollywood, Hong Kong, and Tokyo when it really meant something to be something—an envisioned portrait of what you wanted to represent.

Now, the earth is empty. People struggle to survive. And, all they/the people seem to do is to criticize what they disagree with and what they, themselves, do not like. It is a lost culture/a vacant mindset defined by no art and no inner understanding.

So, to the anyway of the anyway… I suggest that you take a moment and look at your life—take a moment and look at your style or the lack thereof, and then look to the points in history when style was everything and question (to yourself) who and what are you? What are you emulating by what you are saying, what you are doing, what you are wearing, and what you are projecting to the rest of the world? Do you have any style? Do you have a style worth remembering? Is there any art in what you are doing?

Kickboxing Christ
29/Nov/2017 04:16 PM

On a lighter note…

Like most filmmakers, I have come up with a number of ideas for films that have never made it from the page to the stage. Back in the early to mid 90s I had this idea to do a film, Kickboxing Christ or maybe spelled, Kickboxing Khrist. The basic premise was that Jesus came back and instead of initially being a carpenter he was a kickboxer. Though the idea had a high concept, it was one of those films that was going to need a bit of money to pull off as it would need some stages, some sets, and a fairly big cast to sell the whole storyline.

Back when I was working with DGJ, him being a strong Christian, (especially in his latter days), he really like the idea and wanted to pursue it. This was good as Don had access to a lot of production money from a company that would finance his films. The only problem was, Don's mind was a complete cluster fuck. Him getting anything actually done was near impossible. So, I fully developed the story but it never happened.

A few years later, in the early 2000s, I was teaching a class at U.C.L.A. and I got to be friends with one of my older students. He was a mobbed-up guy on the Armenian tip. Like most Armenians, he was very religious and he wanted to do a film about Jesus. I guess he, knowing I was an actor and due to the way I looked: my hair, etc., he asked me about doing a Jesus based film with him. I told him about my idea for Kickboxing Christ. He liked the idea but wanted to make sure that it would be a, *"Serious,"* film.

As he was mobbed-up, he had a lot of money behind him and he could have easily financed such a film to the degree where it would have had some great production value. But, though the offer was tempting, most people who invest in films expect there to be a large return for their investment. This, due to all the BS and hype that is out. The fact is, most indie films, especially if they cost a lot of money to make, do not make a profit. And, I just didn't want to piss off the Armenian mob. So, I turned the offer down.

But, the thought of the film came to mind today as I was taking a moment and having a Venti Flat White at Starbucks this afternoon. So, I thought I would throw it out there to you. If nothing else, you can envision it and play the imaginary movie in your mind. Enjoy it. ☺

* * *
29/Nov/2017 07:43 AM

Before you believe anything, look at who is saying what and question why they are saying it in the first place.

*   *   *

29/Nov/2017 07:41 AM

The people that have been judged the harshest are the ones who become the most judgmental.

You Can't Help Everybody
28/Nov/2017 07:50 AM

I forever find it interesting how people are constantly seeking out people that they believe can and will help them. Whether it is people that will help them get the things that they want, (whatever those things may be), help them with their career, on up to asking god to help them with whatever. People want help. They seek out people that they believe will help them.

This process, by its very nature, is not a bad process as we each need guidance in getting from here to there. But, there becomes a very different mental landscape in this process as people quickly begin to expect things from those they seek help from.

How many times have you witnessed one person being attracted to another person due to what they know or what they have? How many times have you watched as one person attaches themselves to another person due to what they know or what they have? But then, that person begins to expect to be given certain things and to be treated in a specific manner. If they are not then they begin to criticize the person who they once approached. *"Thank you,"* rarely, if ever, enters into the equation. And, that is/this all is a mistake.

This practice is very common with family members when one has more money than another. One has, the other expects. But, why should anybody give anyone anything that they have not earned? And, this is where the whole process falls into eternal complication... People who want, know what they want—they expect to receive what they want. But, when they do not, they become disappointed. When they are treated as less than an equal, (which is the way they should be treated), they become frustrated, angered, and derogatory. Thus, all kinds of interpersonal chaos becomes invoked.

Yet, people constantly seek out others to help them. Why is this? Because they want to be more. They want to be what another person is. They want to possess what another person possesses. The problem with this entire process is, however, no matter how hard you try, you will never be what another person is. You may become less, you may become more, but you will never have what they have—you will never possess their unique understanding because they are they and you are you.

So, as you pass through life, in your process of becoming, you really need to be consciously careful in who you seek out to help you and why you seek them out in the first place. If all you want is to have what they have, do what they do, then you will never achieve that end goal. As you are not them and you can never be them.

Moreover, and from the other side of the subject, some people place themselves in a position where they pretend that they are someone worth asking for help—they are someone that people should seek out. First of all, if someone is behaving in this manner, run the other way. Because all they are is an ego driven entity and there will be a price to pay for your association with them—they may even ask for a specific price to be paid.

Remember, all of this… All of this wanting to be… All of this wanting to have is based upon you wanting to be more than you already are.

In life, we all must find a way to survive; just as our entire existence is based upon desire. This being said, if you seek out others to make you who they are, to make you become who you want to be, there will forever be a loss in who you actually are and a price you must pay to that person for them taking you under their wing.

You being you—you becoming you, you are free. You seeking help from someone/anyone else, there will always be a price to pay and if you do not pay it, if you respond with anger for you not getting what <u>you</u> thought <u>you</u> wanted, all you have done is to create a never ending pattern of retaliatory karma, as one thing always leads to another.

You asked for help. You received help, (to whatever degree), then you didn't like the help you asked for. What is the commonality of this equation? You wanting something.

If you want: if you want to become something; if you want to do what someone else is accomplishing, all you are actually doing is projecting your beliefs about how it will feel to be in the position of that other person who is doing what you think you want to do. Meaning, it is not real. It is only what you think it is. As such, it will never be all that you thought it would be. Thus, in your process of being, if you ask for help, appreciate any help you receive and the person who gave it to you; never blame them for what you become as what you become is only defined by what you envisioned and fantasied in your mind.

You asked for help. Appreciate any help you receive. As you ask, so shall you receive.

* * *

28/Nov/2017 06:43 AM

If you are not saying something positive you are saying something negative.

If you are saying something negative you are hindering the existence of that which you speak.

If you are hampering anything, what do you believe will be the result? The answer; negative karma being focused your direction.

People who embrace the negative, no matter what their justification, always wonder why unwanted events seek them out. The answer is obvious.

Think about what you say. Think about what you do.

Control what you say. Control what you do.

Because the consequences are all around.

Meditation on Time
27/Nov/2017 06:40 AM

Sit down in front of a digital clock. As you sit down, take notice of what time it is. Once you are seated, close your eyes and take a few moments to calm your mind and find your center. Once you feel that you are ready, open your eyes. What time is it now? How much time has passed since you closed your eyes? How do you feel about those moment that are gone?

Now, with your eyes remaining open, watch the clock. Don't stare. Don't allow your eyes to become transfixed so your vision will become blurry. Simply casually watch the clock. Witness the minutes as they change on the face of the clock. As each minute passes, how does that make you feel?

Each minute of your life that passes will be the last time you can experience that minute. How you live each minute of your life comes to define your entire life. Each minute is a whole unit and entity onto itself. By observing a minute, you come to understand how you are feeling and the way in which you are encountering life in that minute. By consciously taking yourself into each minute—by consciously causing your mind to focus on a specific minute, (one minute at a time), you will come to understand the refined nature of the passing of time and how it affects your life specifically. Therefore, by consciously studying the passing of each minute, you will learn to gain control over how your mind processes time and it will teach you how to make the most of each minute of your life.

Sit down. Watch the minutes pass by on a digital clock.

* * *

27/Nov/2017 06:38 AM

What you believe and what is actually the truth may be two very different things.

* * *
26/Nov/2017 07:45 AM

If you don't sell anything you won't have any dissatisfied customers.

When You've Had Enough
25/Nov/2017 12:46 PM

In life, we each reach a point when we've had enough. We don't like something someone or something has done to us and we simply become feed up. When this is a person-to-person relationship, (someone you are close to and you personally know), you can tell them how you feel and hopefully they will listen to your words, understand your feelings, and change the way they are behaving. When it is someone or something OUT THERE this becomes a much more complicated subject.

The thing is, and the thing to really study about yourself when you come to embrace this feeling is, why are you feeling what? In some cases, you are simply mad at yourself or at your life. You may be unhappy with your life, your life's direction, the cards life has dealt you, and so on. Then, no matter what you say to any body or any thing—no matter how they respond, it will not quench your thirst for a difference as what is taking place is taken place solely within you.

In association with this style of behavior, a lot of times you will see people lashing out at TV, radio, political, or sports personalities. They rage and rage but to what end? It equals nothing but making themselves more enraged and unhappy. If you don't like what someone is saying, change the channel. If you don't like how someone is playing, follow another team. If you don't like a book you are reading, close the pages and donate it to your local library.

On the other side of the issues, there are the times when people (and I use the term, *"People,"* in the larger sense), are doing something directly to you that is having a negative impact. Maybe it is an auto shop that supposed fixed your car only to break something else. Maybe you are receiving really bad service from a business. Maybe you bought something online and the description turned out to be fraudulent, and so on… Sometimes people are nice, honest, and sorry they made a mistake and work with you to make it better. Other times people fall back into their arrogance, denial, or the protection of being part of a larger organizational whole and disregard your complaints altogether. Then, you become mad—you've had enough!

The thing is, there are always things you can do in these modern times. Whether it is to write a review on Yelp or even take them to court. The problem with each of these actions is, however, these actions create conflict. And, whenever conflict is created there will be a winner and a loser. Plus, during the process of this process, there will be a lot of emotional damage created. Possibly to their life but assuredly to yours, as you are the one instigating the retaliatory action. Now, I am not saying let people get away with it. I am just saying that there will be a price to pay. …A price to pay for the process of you unleashing your unhappiness with a specific person or place out onto the masses.

This is why so many people love the internet. They can say or do anything anonymously and not be held to task over the truth or the lies of their words. But, is there any honor in this? Is there any redemption? No. It is simply the unleashing of directed or misplaced dissatisfaction.

If we can step back for a moment here, let's look at the bigger picture... Why are you unhappy with something that you bought? Why are you unhappy with someplace that you went? The end-all answer is, and the fact that you must understand, is that you made a choice to buy it, you made a choice to go there. So yes, you may hate what you received for the money you paid but it was you, (due to whatever logic and reason), that made the choice to take that ride. So, who is ultimately to blame?

Do you ever think about this before you become angry at the items you purchased or the services your received? Think about it, you are part of the equation, which makes you at least partially to blame.

Now, you may not like that statement. But, you cannot deny that it is true.

So, here's the thing... You really need to check your desires, check your reasons for doing anything that you do, and really analyze the possible consequences: the good, the bad, and the ugly of any possibility that may occur before you do anything that you do. Why? Because it may equal you having had enough. But, then what? Then, a whole new world of disruption may be invoked.

Are you really willing and able to pay the price for creating a place where you will encounter dissatisfaction?

* * *
23/Nov/2017 06:44 AM

Success breeds arrogance.

Arrogance breeds failure.

* * *

21/Nov/2017 09:35 AM

There is no absolute truth in belief.

There is only the belief of what you believe in.

* * *
21/Nov/2017 09:33 AM

Does your opinion matter when your opinion has no basis in fact?

*   *   *

21/Nov/2017 09:31 AM

Everybody want to blame everyone else but no one wants to blame themselves.

If you are a part of the equation you are at least partially to blame.

Poetry Never Read
21/Nov/2017 07:14 AM

How many of you out there write poetry? How many of you out there draw or paint? How many of you out there play the guitar or the piano? How many of you out there want to write a novel? How many of you out there want to make a movie?

In each of us there is an artist. There is the person who desires to create. For some, this is a very strong desire which causes us to write poetry and short stories, paint paintings, and make music or movies. But, how much of that poetry is ever read by anyone but the author. How many people ever see and appreciate the drawings? How many people ever hear the music?

In life, many people have the dream to have their poetry read by the masses, their music heard, their movies seen. They have the desire to be able to make a living based upon their art. But, very-very few ever find this hidden pathway. Most, can never find the way to live their dream of acceptance of their art. Thus, their writings, their drawings, their music is lost to the veiled realm of the never-never only known of and read by the composer and/or maybe a few close confidants. Is their art any less? No. But, it is not a pathway to a greater expression.

Most, write poetry or create art only when they are young and leave it behind for the reality of making a living as their youth fades away. The man who became understood to be a great and respected poet, Rimbaud, only wrote in his teenage years. The most common reason for this is not that their art and their creativity left them but that their art was not nurtured and developed as it found no audience.

So, who out there writes poetry? Who out there paints and draws? Who out there plays music? Who out there makes movies?

Who out there used to write poetry but does no more? Who out there used to paint or draw but does no more? Who out there used to play music but does no more? Who out there dreamed of being a filmmaker but gave up that aspiration?

There is no pathway for the unheard to be heard. There is no drug to take that will make a person hold onto their art and continue to create when their art has found no audience. There is no magic wand that will provide a person with the money they need to survive if they cannot make a living via their dream of acceptance of their creations. This is life and those are the facts. But, is a poem unread any less a poem? No. It is every bit the art as created by Rimbaud. It is simply silent in the mind of the masses making it an expression of true Zen.

Never stop being creative.

* * *
20/Nov/2017 05:37 PM

Have you ever noticed that the people who want to discredit and destroy others by their words and by the actions ultimately destroy themselves?

*   *   *

20/Nov/2017 11:11 AM

Have you ever had the experience where someone told you something about somebody and you believed them only to find out years later that what they told you was a lie?

Dissatisfaction
20/Nov/2017 07:30 AM

Satisfaction is defined by a sense of embraced contentment. Dissatisfaction is signaled by a state unharmonious angst. Satisfaction leads to a state of heightened awareness not only by the person who is engulfed by this state of mind but by all those they encounter. Dissatisfaction leads the person defined by this responsive emotional life definition and all those people they encounter into a mindset of antagonism, resentment, and unleashing this negative emotion onto the world.

Dissatisfaction is a state of mind. It is not unnatural in that all emotions are simply the way an individual expresses what they are feeling based upon what they have experienced in life. Though dissatisfaction is not unnatural, it is a negative emotion and all undesirable emotions embraced by an individual will cause them to encounter life and act in a less than acceptable manner leading to a life further unfulfilled and defined by ongoing disappointment, frustration, and dissatisfaction.

What is the root of dissatisfaction? It begins in one of two ways. The first is that an individual was treated badly by those around them and they have come to see the world as a hostile place. The second source for developing a mind dissatisfied come from desire—some one wants some thing that they have not achieved or received. Thus, they choose to enter into a mental space of angered displeasure abased upon their own lack of accomplishment. Though the source for their lack of achievement may, in fact, be external, it is they themselves who chooses how they behavior once this understanding has been conceptualized.

This takes us to the source of dissatisfaction. It is a personal choice. It is what one person chooses to do with their personal life experiences and the personal life emotions they have encountered based upon the aspirations they hold for their life. Whereas one person will choose to use negative life experiences as a learning tool and a growing experience, others will use them as a reason to develop undefined anger, leading to the out reaching, ongoing hurting of themselves and others based upon their own internal dissatisfaction.

Dissatisfaction is a personal choice. As all emotions are, it is a feeling felt only by one person. Though emotions can only be felt and experienced by one person, this is not to say that those who hold a commonality of emotional definitions will not find one another and form into a coalition. From this, large amounts of art may be created, just as large amounts of devastation may be instigated. Like attracts like.

Dissatisfaction is an unhealthy emotion. Though some may claim that it is an emotion that may be used as a catalysis to instigate change—as it is a negative emotion all that will be born from it can only emulate as negativity. Moreover, most people do not use this emotion as a motivation for change. Instead, they simply dwell in it and by doing so this does not allow them to accomplish anything with their life but instead simply spread their internalized negativity outwards from their internal being.

As dissatisfaction is an emotion, and as all emotion are a choice, you can choose to consciously and perhaps even forcefully re-alter your thought process and think and feel in a new, better, and more productive manner.

Dissatisfaction does not lead you towards the betterment of anything. It does not cause you to become a better person. If you are engulfed with this emotion, it is only you who can choose to change it. Rethink how you think. Make you and the world a better place.

Same Rhyme Different Song
18/Nov/2017 07:25 AM

The one thing that is sure, if you live in L.A. like I do, you are going to do a lot of driving. It's a big city and unless you possess agoraphobia you are going to need to get from place to place. During that time one of the main things to do is to listen to music on the radio, CDs (remember those?), and/or downloads on your phone. Me too, I do that. As I have very eclectic musical tastes, I listen to a wide range of music styles. One of the things I always notice, throughout all of the music genera's, is that there are so many songwriters using the same combination of words, equaling the same rhyme, in songs all across musical styles, that it is uncanny. The same words, telling the same story, but calling it by a different title.

If we look across the world, it is very much the same. For some reason, many a songwriter has come to believe that the words in a song must rhyme. Now, what rhymes in English doesn't rhyme in Japanese but the concept is the same. Same words, different language, telling a story that has already been told.

World culture is like this, as well. Yes, each culture across the globe has its own unique way of encountering and interacting with life and people. Some cultures are nicer and more respectful; others are more rude and dismissive. But, there is more commonality among world peoples than there are differences. Everyone basically wants the same thing. To be happy, to live a good life, to not encounter too much strife, and so on… Think about it, how different are you than that person you know and like? How different are you than that person you know and hate? You may have a slightly different mental framework. You may like certain things more than one another. You may react to life and people a bit differently. But, how truly different are you?

It is very easy in life to fall into the mix and say the same words the same way as someone/everyone else. You may even do this while labeling what you are saying with a new title. But, how different are you? How different are you than your parents, your grandparents, the person who lives across the street from you? Are you not saying the same things, doing the same things, but simply putting a different label on it?

Uniqueness is only defined in the mind of the individual. Another person, who cannot witness what you view as unique about yourself, will only see you as an, *"Everybody else."* Good or bad, this is life. People are defined by how they fit into the Whole of the All. How do you fit in? And, just how different is what you say, what you do, and how you act?

*   *   *

17/Nov/2017 07:11 AM

Are you looking for a reason to find fault or are you looking for a reason to discover wisdom?

*   *   *
17/Nov/2017 06:38 AM

Why is it that when you dream a dream too long it all becomes weird, it all goes wrong?

* * *
16/Nov/2017 05:23 PM

If you have hurt someone's life, you are forever defined by that one action.

Do You Have a Conscience?
14/Nov/2017 12:57 PM

Okay... You've done something wrong. You did something that hurt someone else. Maybe you took something from them, maybe you lied to them, maybe you abused them, maybe you harshly judged them, maybe you did something that affected their life progression or the next step that they were going to take in life, or maybe you just said something that hurt their feelings. Now what? And, do you care?

Most people have a caring heart. They care about the people they love, the people they like, and the people they respect. Some even care about the greater whole of humanity. They live their life trying to never hurt anyone and helping as many people as possible. These are the people that we should emulate.

There is, however, another group of people. There are those who consciously hurt others—take things from them, cause damage to their life and once they perform these actions, they do not care. They do not try to right any damage they have created. Maybe, they even attempt to find a justification for what they did. But, the key to this equation is who instigated the action? Who was the first person to do some-thing? That is the person responsible. That is the person to blame. Reaction is only an action based upon response. If you stole, if you hurt, if you lied, if you judged, you are the responsible party. Again, now what? And, do you care?

As we pass through life we will encounter many different types of people. Some will be happy, joyous, good, and thankful. Others will be hurtful, spiteful, jealous, and judgmental. Who we become is dominated not only by who and what we choose to be but by whom we associate with—the type of person we allow in our presence. Thus, we must learn to look for the telltale signs of who and what a person truly is. Do they have a conscience? Because if they don't, they have the potential to hurt our life and the life of others and do so without caring. And if, we associate with this type of person, if we are their friend, we are as much responsible for any of their actions as they are, as we have allowed them to perform these actions, with no reprisals.

Do you have a conscience? Do the people you know; the people you like and love have a conscience?

What will your actions equal in the lives of others? What will the actions of the people you know equal in the lives of others? It is essential to look at this question. It is essential that not only do you chart a conscious course for your own life but that you only associate with people that also consciously set about on a path of living a good life, doing good things, and hurting no one for any reason.

Been There Done That
13/Nov/2017 09:05 AM

Have you ever had the experience where someone comes up to you and they are so excited about something that they are doing? Due to the fact that they are so excited, they want to bring you into their project. Maybe they think that because you used to do something similar, that you will be as excited as they are. But, you are not. Why? Because you've been there and you've done that and you've moved on.

I forever find it interesting when this happens to me, especially in the film industry. Due to the fact that, once-upon-a-time, I was the king of doing things on a no-budget budget, people believe that is still who I am. They invite me—they want me to go to their sets and watch them steal a location or setup a great backdrop for a shot without getting any filming permits, production insurance, or anything like that. Sure... That's great! I did that more times than I can even remember. But, it is essential to note, when I was doing my Zen Films on that level, I was never really excited about it. I was never enthralled with the getting over on someone or something or society in general. For me, it was always about getting the best project out there that could be had. It was about the endgame not about the doing. In fact, I really did not like that part of the no-budget filmmaking process, as it equaled too much paranoia.

Now, for anyone who has ever made a low or no budget film, you can immediately attest to the fact that your film will find many a critic. But, how many of those people have gone out there and actually made a film? Few, I would wager. Yet, they voice their tone of hatred to the world. But, people do that all the time. As I so often discuss in this blog, there is a certain type of person who looks for something or someone not to like. They do not seek the positive, they do not attempt to find the good in the lacking, all they want to do is expel their inner demons onto the vastness of society. Bad! That is just the wrong way to live.

But, for all of those people out there who want to create, who are trying to create, who are doing whatever it takes to create, I salute you. Maybe you will be the one to make something truly great and long-lasting that will change the all and the everything. If not, at least you tried.

For me, as a filmmaker, as I have shifted my focus to the more surreal realms of cinema over the past decade, the Non-Narrative Zen Films as I have titled them, I have held onto to the essence expressed in the doctrines of Zen Filmmaking that I formulated—of just getting out there and doing it. But, in this doing, my focus has shifted to the visually abstract. And, from this and within this, I have created some Zen Film Mind Rides that I really like, while others I have created, I just do not like that much. Just as at the root of my character driven films, some turn out better than others. Currently, I am simply enjoying creating visual images without the need for personality—not mine, not others.

So, when that person who loves what I have done in the past wants to take me into their excitement, it makes me happy that they are happy. It makes me happy that they are creating. But me, I'm walking a different path these days. I prefer the silent and the abstract, lost to the realms of its own visual suchness, compare to the driven that is attempting to piece the veil of commonality. A place I never truly understood.

The Honesty of Your Words
10/Nov/2017 08:16 AM

What you say defines who you are. What you say about others defines who they are—at least in the minds of those who listen to your words.

What you say defines how you think. The way you say what you say defines your psychological mindset.

What you say and the way you say it provides a view into how you think. What you say about people defines what you believe about people. What you say about the world defines what you believe about the world.

Do you ever think about what you say before you say it? Do you ever consider the overriding implications of your speech?

Is what you say always true? Or, is what you say simply based upon what you believe in any given moment of time defined by your own current set of standards and desires?

Do you want people to believe what you say? If so, why?

How does what you say affect the way the world views you?

How does what you say affect the people and the things you talk about?

When you make a mistake in what you say do you correct yourself or does your ego and your desire to be seen as a knower keep your from undoing your wrong?

Do you ever consider the karmic implications of how what you say will affect your own life and the lives of those you discuss?

Life is a complicated interaction of personal judgments claimed to be understandings and/or truths. But, what are your understandings and your truths based upon? Are they based upon fact or are they based upon your personal judgment? If it is the ladder, what you are saying has no basis in truth; it only has a basis in judgment.

How often, when you realize that you were wrong in what you said, do you correct the statement that you made? If you don't, that means you define your life from a perspective of no personal assessments—you said it and that is that. If you are not whole enough onto yourself to correct false words spoken, the true words you speak will eventually be seen to be lies.

Verbal conversation defines much of our human interaction. If what you say is not based upon the truth then anything that you say is a lie and, thus, the lie spreads from you.

How many times have you told a lie? How many times has what you believed to be true turned out not to be true. Do you ever correct what you say? If you don't that says a lot about who and what you truly are.

Enlightenment Through the Arts
09/Nov/2017 07:49 AM

The other night I was watching a production called, Unseen Cinema, on TCM. What this program presented was short films that were created in the early years of filmmaking that truly pushed the boundaries of what was then considered mainstream filmmaking. Obviously, this was right up my alley. ☺

One of the films they presented was a 1924 piece titled, *Ballet Mecanique.* I had not seen this film in many-many years. But, as I again watched it, I was reminded what a groundbreaking piece of cinema it truly was—especially for 1924. Had it been done in the 1960s, it would have been expected. If it was done in that era it may have been called an, *"Acid Flick,"* as by then LSD was a common thread that avant-garde filmmakers embraced. But, it was made long before LSD was even invented. It is an amazing piece of cinema. What motivated the filmmaker(s) to make this piece, I can only imagine. Watch it if you can. It is inspiring.

Way back then, like now, there was a mainstream that permeated society. There was the accepted norm. Even though cinema was a fairly new art form infiltrating society, there was already a small group of filmmakers who were pushing its boundaries to new and unexplored levels. Most of these people did not find a large audience. Yet, they had an artistic and a spiritual purpose in all that they did. Thus, it rose to the level of true art.

Most people, especially in an art form like filmmaking, do what they do inspired by a desire for fame, recognition, and/or monetary reward.

Think about the majority of people that enter the field of filmmaking as actors and filmmakers. Why do they do it? It is not for the art. It is for the ego, the fame, the perks, and the money. The stories I could tell you...

How many people do what they do solely as a means to create art? How many people live their life by that code? Very few.

After that program was over, I flipped the channels and, amazingly, I happened upon a documentary on the great jazz musician John Coltrane broadcast on a PBS station. Immediately, the deep inspiration of this man's music struck me. If you have not listened to John Coltrane you are really missing out. He was a master of unparalleled talent. Even though in my early years I was never a fan of the sax, he is the whole reason I bought a sax and took it up in my early twenties. When I did the soundtrack for the original (not the wide release) version of Samurai Johnny Frankenstein I based my sax playing on his style—though it was a poor imitation. But, what Coltrane did was artfully amazing. You should really listen to him. It is magic.

The documentary took the viewer through his life up to his death. In his later years, he married the musician Alice (McLoud) Coltrane. I knew her. It was fun to be reminded. How I met her is after the passing of Coltrane, in grief, she became a disciple of my teacher, Swami Satchidananda. But, at some point in the 1970s she had an interpersonal revelation and she anointed herself, Swami Turiyasangitananda. From this she began wearing the traditional orange robes of the sanyass order and the like.

There is no disrespect meant in this next statement, on any level, but I clearly remember this one time when we had gone with Gurudev to LAX to see him off and Turiyasangitananda was flying with him. She was there with her orange robes, big smile, and big personality. He looked to a few of us disciples and said, *"She's gone a little crazy, hasn't she?"* This was just after her transformation. But, the fact is, she found her wisdom and her art in her own way. And, this is something that she never left behind. I remember on late night TV, back in the days of UHF, she had a late-night TV show, on one of those poorly broadcast networks, where she would chant with a harmonium. She spent the rest of her life teaching and chanting at a spiritual center she created. Art, equaling spiritually, by her own definition.

And, this is the crux of the point, the people that push the boundaries of human understanding and acceptance are the ones who take the chances—do the unexpected and the unseen. Most people pass through their life based upon a precept of preconceived judgment. But, what comes from that? Nothing. Nothing new is enacted, created, and no one is inspired. But, the few who stretch the limits of the accepted norm, they are the ones who inspire change and spiritual enlightenment throughout time, space, and society.

* * *
07/Nov/2017 03:41 PM

Before you can be a savior you have to save yourself.

The Things They Will Never Know
06/Nov/2017 07:01 AM

How much of your Life Time do you spend consciously doing things for other people?

How many of the things that you actually do for other people would you do if they did not know you were doing them?

Do you only do things for other people when they either acknowledge that they know what you are doing, show thanks for what you are doing, or you remind them of the fact that you are doing something for them?

Most people, in the space of their life, do things for themselves. When they do things for other people, they generally have an endgame result in mind that will positively affect their own life; which is their sole motivation for doing anything that they are doing in the first place.

How do you operate your life? How much of your Life Time do you spend attempting to make things better for someone else? How much of what you do would you do if you received no acknowledgement, thanks, or payment for the actions you have enacted?

Have you ever actually gone out of your way, made a plan, did something positive for someone, and you never alerted that person to the fact that you actually instigated a plan, saw it through to its completion, and never asked for any acknowledgement or compensation?

Most people operate their life from a very selfish space. Do you? How much of your Life Time do you spend stepping outside of what you want, what you desire, and set about on a course that will make a positive difference in another person's life even if it is a very small thing that they never even knew that you did? You should try it.

* * *
06/Nov/2017 07:00 AM

Desperation breeds desperate acts.

* * *
05/Nov/2017 06:54 AM

It's true, you can't control other people. But, you can control yourself.

Thus, don't do anything that creates a situation where another person is motivated or instigated into doing something negative based upon your words or your actions.

* * *
05/Nov/2017 06:52 AM

Just as all culture is defined by the greater whole of its people, so too is a specific religion.

If your religion is doing bad things to people or places you are a part of that negative act as you are supportive of that religion. Thus, you too will be held responsible.

Roller Blade Seven: The Unseen Scenes
05/Nov/2017 06:45 AM

As I have discussed a million times, it forever amazes me the amount of discourse and discussion that continues to take place around the first Zen Film, *The Roller Blade Seven*. What I am also always amazed about is the fact that people continue to come to all kinds of conclusions about the film. And sure, I'm right there with you, it is a weird and bizarre movie. But, as I have said a million times, whatever Donald G. Jackson and I did by creating that film over twenty-five years ago, we did something right, as it is still at the forefront of discussion.

All this being said, the amount of unfounded discussion that takes place around this film continually reminds me about how people like to come to all kinds of conclusions about everything and then spout their supposed wisdom out to the world but they do this without ever basing anything they are saying upon actual fact. They don't know, yet they speculate and talk and talk and talk.

Understanding all the things that are told to me by and about what people think and say about the film, I clearly understand they have never researched the facts about the film. Just one example it the Zen Documentary I made about the movie, *Roller Blade Seven: The Unseen Scenes*. I mean there is so much dialogue about what went into the creation of the movie, behind the scenes interviews, and yes, unseen scenes, that I find it very interesting that all of these people discuss *Roller Blade Seven,* but they do so without ever having watched that film. ...Or, they discuss the movie without having viewed the books, Zen

Filmmaking, where there is a chapter devoted to the film or *Roller Blade Seven: A Photographic Exploration* which also provides deep insight into the film's creation and metaphysical mindset via photographs.

I guess what I am saying here, and these goes to all levels of life, if you don't know, you don't know. And, if what you are saying is based upon not-knowing, all you are doing is spreading lies out to the world while presenting them as facts. And, this certainly goes to all levels of life. I'm just using *The Roller Blade Seven* as an example.

In life, in many cases, the essence of knowledge, where it all came from and how it started, is not available. But, in other cases, you can go to the source, you can learn the actual goings-on, leading to you comprehending the factual truth. Then, at least, what you think and what you say, based upon what you believe, will have some level of authenticity.

Go to the source—study the source. This is the only way to speak the truth.

You Messed Up. Now What?
03/Nov/2017 09:30 AM

Have you ever had the experience of choosing to do something and after you did it you realize that you really messed up—you shouldn't have done it. But, you did do it. Now what? What do you do?

What you choose to do defines your life. What you choose to do after the fact of experiencing the results of what you chose to do defines you as a person.

I believe that each of us has made a choice to do something, as we have passed through life, that we later realized was a mistake. Some of these comprehensions are immediate while others are realized over time. But, we chose to do it. Later, we realized that by doing it we messed up. Now what can we do?

Each person reacts to their life mistakes differently. By studying how a person reacts is a true window into their soul. Some people immediately own their mistake. They take responsibility for them. They try to fix them. Others adamantly deny their responsibility in the situation to the very end. They attempt to blame someone else for doing what they, personally, chose to do. Most people fall somewhere in between. But, the ultimate truth of life is that you chose to do something, whether it turned out great or horrible is all on you. What are you going to do now?

The age-old adage that it is impossible to fix something once it is broken is very true. But, knowing this, does that allow you to have a justification to not even try to fix it? Many follow this path. What is done is done and all be damned

This is especially the case of the choice that was made affected some other person in a much more negative manner than the person who actually instigated the deed. *"Their problem, not mine."* Think about it, is that how you react?

In other cases, a mistake that was made may truly affect the doer in all kinds of negative ways. Then what? Then what do you do? Do you only try to fix it when you are forced to try to fix it? Or, do you simply live in denial about its ongoing consequences? Because that is the case, a poorly made choice has the potential to affect you forever if you do not stop its emancipation.

It is plain to see that all life is a choice—all that you live is defined by the choices that you have previously made. Thus, you really need to look to the causation factor for what makes you make the choices that you make. Do you do that? Or, do you simply pass through life blindly experiencing the emotional ecstasy or the despair? Moreover, when you do make a choice that has had a negative effect on you or on someone else, who do you blame?

All life is created at its source point and that source point is you. No matter what is going on outside of you, you are the one who makes the choice to make the choices that you make defined by what choices are available to you. Once you make that choice, you experience the consequences of that choice.

So, what do you do when your choice goes wrong? If you cannot immediately define this, you do not know yourself. If you blame anyone else for the choice(s) that you make you are living in a space of unenlightened selfishness. Own your decision. Love your choices when they were the right decision but never stop until you fix any wrong choice that you have made. This is the way to live a good, whole life.

Know yourself. Understanding your reasons why. Be whole onto yourself. Choose to make the right choice.

My Mother Practiced Voodoo
03/Nov/2017 09:25 AM

Though my mother considered herself a devout Christian, she practiced Voodoo. Or perhaps, more ideally stated, she practiced Hoodoo. She did this without ever calling it by a name.

She would do incantations, use various created objects to be symbolic of people she felt needed to have a specific energy sent their direction, and so on. She was very methodical about what she did. As a young child, who was indoctrinated into the Christian faith as many American children are, I always found this strange, as it didn't seem very Christian to my young mind.

Yes, yes, if we study American history and the evolution of Hoodoo, it shows that the practitioners of Hoodoo, which came to the Americas as African slaves, did place a great emphasis on the bible. But, how is that Christianity?

My mother was also a very superstitious person. If this thing happened she believed it would equal that thing.

Now, I've told this story elsewhere, but one of the occurrences that really drove this point home in my life was when my grandmother died. My mother came home with all of the appropriate tears in her eyes and she told me that as it had rained on her mother's open grave someone else in the family would die within a year. And, she decided it was going to be her. This was one of her families accepted superstations. Throughout that next year she constantly drove that point home, *"I'm going to die. It rained on my mother's grave."* *"Less than a year now and I will be gone."* As a young kid, this obviously really freaked me out. *"Don't die,"* I would exclaim. *"Can't help it, my destiny has been written,"* she would say.

My mother, father, and I were having dinner at a Chinese restaurant on Crenshaw one evening in December of 1968. As is the tradition, we got our fortune cookies at the end of the meal. My mother's cookie had no fortune in it. *"You see, I told you I'm going to die."* My father immediately replied, *"Here, have mine."* He gave her his fortune. He died a week later.

So, was this invocation? I don't know. Was this focused energy being summoned and released? Don't know... Or, was this simply one of the random coincidences of a chaotic life? Will I ever know? Will any of us? I do know that my mother lived for another thirty years and my father did not.

This is an important point to consider as you pass through life. Energy is focusable. Whether you believe in religion or not, superstition or not, mystical powers or not, Voodoo or not, this does not change the fact that energy is focusable. For this reason, what you think about, what you say, what you do, all creates an energy field around you that invokes a specific pattern of energy that will come to be your life's definition. What you think about, you create. What you speak, you create. What are you creating?

What are you thinking about? What actions are you taking based upon those thoughts? What outcomes occur based upon what you are thinking and the actions you are undertaken due to what you are thinking? And, what energy are you creating and how will it affect you and those around you?

Remember, you may love or hate someone or something. You may do what you do to make something happen to you or to them: be that positive or negative. But, whatever emanates from you, you are responsible for. Thus, there is always a karmic price to pay. Be careful what you believe and what your beliefs cause you to invoke.

Helping Helps. Hurting Hurts.
02/Nov/2017 06:26 AM

Recently, it seems that I've spent a lot of time discussing helping in this blog. This has once again been brought into focus with the terrorist attack that recently took place in NYC with the guy renting a truck from Home Depot and running down a bunch of people. BAD! Now, terrorist attacks have gone on throughout history but with the Arab Spring and all of the focus being placed on Radial Islam it has seemingly become a common thread through this period of history.

It is important for all of us to understand that a terrorist attack is not necessary something large like what that man did this week in New York or a massive bomb or cyber-attack, it is also implemented by small things. ...Small things that are designed to hurt someone or something. So, depending on how you behave; what you say and what you do, you too may be responsible for terrorist attacks.

As I have said in the past, *"All negative behavior comes from a place of unanswered pain."* What is your unanswered pain? And, do you allow it to control you; guiding you in what you say and what you do?

People who are dominated by internal pain and a lack of internally understood self-fulfillment seek out others of this same mindset. And, they are easy to find. Who among us did not have some bit of harshness hurt us somewhere in our life? But, do you allow that person who did that or that moment in your life where your felt it to define who you have become? Or, have you chosen to consciously rise above it and be more?

If it is the previous, then you seek out, are drawn to, and associate with those who will amplify a negative mindset within you. If this is the case, the path you walk in life is set up to hurt people. If you do follow this path, there is nothing that I, or anyone else, can say that will change your ideology because your sense of purposed is based in the negativity of the adrenaline you feel from focusing your mind on this energy. It is very addictive. It is only if you choose to change that you can actually change.

Most people are not focused on the hurting of others, however. They are focused on living their life. They don't have time for it. But, the hurting of other people begins in small ways. It is initially orchestrated by what you are guided to think by those around you—the way you are guided to think. This is where this mindset takes shape. But, it is from that mental place that people then personally begin to adopt and practice this essence of the negative. They do this by how they speak, write, and act. This is where the terrorism is born. These small things are the beginning of the larger terrorist act.

Okay, all this being said, think about this, *"How does it feel when you have been hurt?"* It hurts; right? It doesn't feel good. Why would you want to do that to anyone else? Why would you want them to feel pain? If you are so lost in your own unanswered pain, this should be the motivation for you to look outside of yourself and seek solace from a source of positivity. Just like those who invoke the negative; those people and those organizations that embrace the positive are out there, as well.

Now, think about how does it feel when somebody says something nice about you or does something nice for you—maybe they help you out when you need so help? It feels pretty good; right?

So, who do you want to be, a conduit for help and goodness or someone who invokes harm and negativity? Think about it and then act upon it. Helping, helps. Hurting, hurts. The one is obviously better than the other.

Grinding Your Own Coffee
01/Nov/2017 07:24 AM

What you do as you pass through life will come to define your life.

You have a choice as to what you do as you pass through life.

Your life is defined by what you have chosen to do as you have passed through your life.

Life is an interesting conglomeration of definitions orchestrated by where you find yourself in time and in space. Once you come to understand where you are, you are then allowed to make choices as to what you will do, defined by your definition(s). Some of these are large decisions that will come to define the larger, overall you. Other of these choices are small decisions that will illustrated the inner you. In either case, your choice(s) define you. Thus, you need to be careful in deciding what you will do as what you choose to do sets the ALL of your life into motion.

In the 1980s things began to change in the United States. Items like coffee grinders began to be offered to the masses. This was a noticeable change in that throughout the 1950s, 1960s, and 1970s the focus was on taking as much of the do-ing away from people as possible. Born were TV dinners, frozen pizzas, instant coffee, and microwaves ovens. Then, people didn't want to do, they wanted it to be done.

As times changed, people wanted to return to a more organic and controlled lifestyle. They wanted to buy whole coffee beans and grind their own coffee. Me too. I bought a coffee grinder when they were first made available to the general public. And wow, compared to today's prices, they were expensive. But, it was fun. It was like in the Zen Tea Ceremony, it was a meditation. Making the conscious choice to control and to take power over what you (I) were about to drink.

This trend has continued into the twenty-first century. Hand-in-hand with this, all of the easy-do stuff has also improved. The frozen pizza, which once were terrible, evolved into being pretty good.

But, doing is a choice. What you do is a choice. And again, what you do defines your life.

What you do, you do, because you have come to understand that is what you are supposed to do. But, how much time, how much mental energy, do you spend actually analyzing what you choose to do—thus and thereby coming to consciously find the true definition of your life? Most people spend very little time thinking about any of this, they just do. And, this is what sets the life lived consciously apart from the life just lived without true living.

Your childhood, how you grow up and where you grow up, will come to define much of whom you can and will evolve into becoming. As a child, I used to witness the comparison between my mother and my father. My father, who grew up in Los Angeles, was always on the cutting edge of understanding. My mother, who came from a smaller city in the Midwest, was far more prone to never looking to anything new or different. In fact, she would rebuke all change as long as she could.

I remember when I would occasionally visit her childhood home as a youngster. I was amazed at the fact that they had one of those hand crank washing machines. I mean, it was ancient. Yes, once upon a time it was probably a vast improvement over older methods but that was

351

decades ago. But, my mother, and her siblings, owned that house until the 1990s when they all passed away. Then, the house was bequeathed to me. I sold it—the ancient washing machine included. The washer never changed. They used that ancient method forever. Was it better? I don't know? Was it a process of meditation for them? Doubtful. Or, was it simply what they had come to accept as an understanding and a condition of and for life. Thus, they were so locked into a mindset of, *"That's the way it's supposed to be."* A mindset that they never attempted a change.

How much do you choose to change of the choices you've made?

This takes us to the point of all this. What you do is, at least partially, defined by where and when you came up in history. What you do, defines the you, you choose to become. What you choose to do defines, your life.

What do you choose to do and how do you choose to do it?

Do you make your choices by choice or do you simply allow the known and the expected to define your reality which will then define the definition of your life?

Your life is your choice. What you choose to do not only affect your every living moment but it will also be all that is left when your life is over. What do you choose to do? How do you choose to do it? And, what will be the effect of what you have chosen to do on your life and on the life of others?

May You Live in Interesting Times
31/Oct/2017 04:01 PM

There is the ancient Chinese curse, *"May you live in interesting times."* I guess all of us, living in this day and in this age, have been cursed; as things are very interesting.

I think we can all agree that these, *"Interesting times,"* are predominately defined by and are due to the advent of the internet and social media. The internet is vast. It offers us so many possibilities that were not available just a few years ago. But, it is also damning as people are free to spout off anything that they will—be it true or be it false. What this has led to is a lot of two of the key terms of the day being highly invoked; namely: *"Bullying"* and *"Fake News."* I mean, think about it, people say whatever they want to say on the internet and social media and they pay no price for saying it. There is no justice, there is no law, so anything and everything goes.

There are those of us who attempt to hold fast to a moral high ground, controlling what we say as we understand that our words have wide-spanning implications. One word can create forever karma. But, think about the internet; all of the unsubstantiated accusations—all of the things you read and all the things you believe; all based upon no-one's critical logic, just someone's desired belief. And, forget about the news on the internet; it's just someone's interpretation of what will be disproven tomorrow.

Certainly, there is the good side to all of this, and the internet in general, as we have recently been witness to; i.e., people may be called to task for their bad deeds. But, one of the key elements to this equation is, who among us has not done something bad in their lifetime? Let's remember the elemental Biblical quote from John 8:7, *"So when they continued asking him, he lifted up himself, and said unto them, He that is without sin among you, let him first cast a stone at her."* We all have sinned! Certainly, some of us more than others. But, most of us, as we pass through life, attempt to become better versions of ourselves and sin no more. We attempt to fix what we have broken and help those we have hurt. Do you?

Yet, in this internet world with no justice, how many of you actually practice making yourself better; not judging, not allowing the words you write today to negatively affect someone else's life tomorrow and the next day and the next?

The fact is, so many people say so many things without ever considering the ramifications of what their words will do to the life of another person. Yet, as so many people are lost to the truth of a Higher Self, they find people to believe what they say. And some, in fact, find their sense of self-worth by doing so. From this, universal damage is created across the broad spectrum of reality. And, the truth is, most people don't care. They are unhappy with their life, they are dissatisfied, they are not self-aware or self-actualized so they want everyone to embrace the pain that they feel.

Living life, in this day and age, is interesting; yes. But, it is also complicated. Though life has always been complicated, this fact has been magnified by the amount of people out there who believe that what they say should be heard whether it is true or false.

But remember, one of the key facts to life is that opinion is instigated by one person. Yes, it may spread to others. But, it is sourced at one point.

If your opinion affects the life of someone else, in a negative manner, then your opinion becomes a sin; as it hurts someone else's existence. From this, unless you undo it, never-ending negative karma is born. This is why you really need to think about what you do as you do it, what you say as you say it, and what you believe as you believe it.

So, here we are, living in interesting times; what do we, as conscious, caring individuals do? All we can do is to try to not be dominated by the lack of justice, truth, honesty, and control that exits out there in cyberspace. All we can do is to call out judgment or negative words as negativity when we see it or read it. Counteract it by saying something positively positive. And, be a good person who says and does only good things.

We can all be more. We can all attempt to undo what we have done and hurt no one else along the pathway of our life.

Choose to be more than being controlled by those who are lost to unrefined, unnecessary judgment, and those who wish to inflict pain by their words and their deeds. Write good things. Say good things. Do good things. Be more than being subjugated by the words of others. Be more than being dominated by who you used to be. Be good. Do good. Free yourself from the curse of living in interesting times.

*   *   *

31/Oct/2017 06:24 AM

"What I was thinking then, I am not thinking now."

What happens when your thinking changes?

* * *
28/Oct/2017 08:43 AM

Many times you don't know until you are pushed into knowing.

FADE OUT.

The Zen